GW01270748

FINDING FINAGHY

To Jan,
with all best wishes,
David
(hope we'll all meet up
sometime!)

FINDING FINAGHY

A MEMOIR

DAVID GEPP

LAGAN PRESS
DERRY - LONDONDERRY
2014

Published by
Lagan Press
A Verbal Group Company

Stable Lane & Mall Wall
Bishop Street Within
Derry-Londonderry
BT48 6PU

www.laganpress.co

© David Gepp, 2014

The moral rights of the author have been asserted.

ISBN: 978 1 908188 39 7

Author: Gepp, David
Title: Finding Finaghy
2014

for my parents, Josephine and Samuel Gepp,
who were without bigotry or prejudice

'Love is wise, hatred foolish.'
– Bertrand Russell

One

THERE ARE OLD-FASHIONED SPIRES OF Golden Rod, spreading fertile as weeds, in the sunshine down the side of the garden. A chubby child, with long hair in ringlets, is drawing his cupped hands up the stems, catching the wasps crawling through the flowers. He bends his head forward and chuckles in delight as they crawl out, one by one, between his thumbs, to clean their antennae and fly away. He laughs, throws his hands up, shaking off the others, and moves to another flower.

This child is living in the Garden of Eden. It is a world of sun and light and love. A place where blackcurrants and redcurrants ripen and are made into jams and pies. There are smells of gooseberries and sweet peas. Aunties and uncles come to tea on Sundays, and he has been told that God is Love.

A dawn has come out of the night of a world that was at war just three years before he was born. A dawn in which all things seem bright and beautiful, and he sings:

> 'Way far beyond Jordan
> We'll meet in that land,
> That beautiful land...
> 'Way far beyond Jordan
> We'll meet in that beautiful land.
> If you get there before I do, look out for me
> For I'm coming too.
> 'Way far beyond Jordan
> We'll meet in that beautiful land.

The sunlight comes through the window from the garden behind as he pipes his heart out for Auntie Annie and Uncle John. In that long distant country when he was three, and had a halo of sunlight, and his religion was innocence.

Do you remember flying?

Waiting until the quiet breathing from the other side of the room told you your sister was asleep. And you were free to push back the bedclothes and drift and float around the ceiling. You could roll and swim, and drift downstairs with one hand on the banisters; and float away again on the comforting murmur of grown-up voices.

And, back in bed, in those long midsummer evenings, is there still the distant sound of a lawnmower being pushed back and forth in a neighbouring garden, lulling you to sleep?

This child may be in the Garden of Eden; but others have eaten the fruit of the Knowledge of Good and Evil.

A grown-up calls to him – 'Oh don't do that son, those will sting you!'

'Oh no', the child says, , 'look, I'll show you!'

And, his mind distracted, the wasp stings him.

So he became aware of the power of language – that being told something may sometimes make it so.

But language has positive as well as negative powers. He made this small but important discovery one day as he played by the Michaelmas daisies in the front garden. A man he didn't know was walking past, so the child said, 'Hello', over the low garden wall. The stranger turned his head, smiled, and said, 'Hello!' in return.

He felt sublimely cheered by the outcome of this first simple experiment. *One word* spoken meant an unknown grown-up had paid attention to a small child – and responded with pleasure. The possibilities for speech seemed endless. The prospect delighted me.

One year when I was an infant our parents had taken us to the circus in the King's Hall. At a moment of silent tension, more impressed by the bowel function of an elephant, I had remarked loudly– 'Look at that elephant doing its ninnies, Daddy!'– which amused those around and embarrassed my parents (but not enough to stop them retelling it as I got older).

Some time after, seated with my father on the dark wooden, slatted benches of one of the old cream and blue trams in the city centre, he pointed out that we were passing the City Hall (the seat of local government). Confusing it with the King's Hall, I shouted out, 'Is that where all the clowns are, Daddy?'

A gruff man sitting next to us laughed and said something like, 'Aye, you're right enough there, son.'

There were trams and red trolleybuses running in the city at that time. Trolleybuses sometimes got detached from their overhead power lines and a little street theatre would build up as the traffic jammed and the driver and conductor tried to fix it. They had to pull a long thick bamboo pole, with a hook on top, out of a hole in the back of the bus. This was only possible if the traffic, which still included the odd horse and cart in those days, could be cleared from behind. Then they would wobble about with this great pole, trying to get the twin black connectors, on top of the bus, back onto the power lines again. Most people would stop and watch.

Some days too, opposite the City Hall by Robinson & Cleaver, there was a man sitting on the pavement playing a long saw with a violin bow. He played slow, wistful, wobbly airs. There was a yearning and a melancholy in the sound, which enthralled me.

My father would give me some coppers to put in his cap, while the two men exchanged a few friendly words.

One day we went on down Royal Avenue, and up some flights of dusty old stairs to visit a friend of my father's, a tailor called Paddy Mallon, who sat cross-legged on a table, sewing.

Paddy Mallon was a generous man, who gave me an eye-widening half a crown – a lot of money to a child in those days.

Two

THE VERY FIRST TEARS I SHED, the first howlings after a lost moon, were in Mrs Harper's nursing home at 8 and 10 Mount Charles (pronounced Char-less), Belfast. My mother spent nine days there, at a rate of eight guineas a week, plus sixteen and nine for drugs, and a guinea for theatre fees and dressings. I cost, by the receipt, a grand total of twelve pounds thirteen and ninepence to be born on that day at the end of May 1948. And I've never paid it back.

My friend, Norman Sames, would tell me a few years later that babies come out of women's tummies. So I run to my mother for confirmation. 'Don't be so silly,' she says, 'how could a baby come out of a wee woman like Mrs Sames?' So I talk Norman back to ignorance again.

Maybe it was the memory of the mastitis, or the dressings and the messiness of childbirth, that helped make her evasive, or natural prudery, but my mother would only ever tell us that babies came out of the Doctor's Black Bag (though she would turn up her nose at Gooseberry Bush or Stork stories).

Set against her squeamishness was a sensitivity too, for I remember her telling me that Leonardo da Vinci wouldn't walk on a daisy, so as not to spoil its perfect beauty. She also told us that if the golden 'dust' came off a moth's wings it would not be able to fly, and that we shouldn't catch butterflies in our hands for the same reason.

After my sister and me, she would have no more children.

Carole was four years older, and looked after me when I was an infant in the way of big sisters – in the street, and on our walks to the 'Wee Woods' or the 'Big Woods' or further afield. And in return, if something bad happened, like when I fell down the bank and bloodied my nose on the stones of the railway path near Finaghy Station, I made light of it, and joked that I had fallen in beetroot juice, and that was why my shirt was red – to amuse the grown-ups and distract them from blame.

I think my mother spoiled me more, and Carole, as the girl, had the harder time of it. But I was still started on the washing up, she on the drying up, when we were tall enough to reach the sink.

There are some black and white photographs of us both from around that time. We are perched on the edge of the wooden box our father used to grow his sweet peas in. It is a sunny day, faint shadows of the sweet peas fall on the whitewashed wall behind. Carole has her head down and laughs. She holds her small brother by the hand. He, with short trousers and dimpled knees, has the look of someone who has just said something bold, or silly, or stupid, to make them laugh.

For a long time I have been looking at these small photographs, and for a long time I seemed to be looking at an image of a small person, in another time, with whom I had no connection – other than the acquired knowledge that it was a picture of me. Then, one day I was thinking about this and was quite coincidentally perched on the edge of a wall – with my hands on my knees as they are in the photograph – when my *body* remembered for me. Momentarily I was back as that three-year-old, chubby hands on chubby knees, perched on the box in the back garden, in the sunshine with the scent of the sweet peas. The experience was oddly, and deeply, comforting.

Our father had TB and disappeared from our early lives. Years later (or it may only have been months) when I was just big enough to reach the snib, I was sent to answer a knock at the door. 'Mammy,' I remember calling, 'there's a man at the door for you.' My father, standing there in his grey jacket, must have been hurt to the quick.

The Garden had suffered from my father's absence. The

only thing that remained was an old plum tree that grew like a bush and never had fruit.

It helped make up for the loss of that youthful Paradise that our father now knew how to make French Toast, and Cinnamon Toast, and brought home Gunpowder Tea, and Green Tea and other exotic delights, and quickly became our Daddy and my ideal person again.

He would warm our pyjamas in front of the fire for us, when the weather was cold.

I was puzzled for a long time though about something he said, as we walked down the street one evening, with him holding my hand on our way to the bus stop. There was a big moon, and I asked him what the moon was: 'It's a planet,' he said. But I didn't know that word, so I heard, 'It's a plant.' I pondered to myself for a long time as to where the stem could be, or the pot it was in, before deciding it didn't make any sense at all.

He also had a habit of saying, unexpectedly: 'Mares eat oats and does eat oats and little lambs eat ivy' – which, if you haven't seen it written, sounds funny and rhythmic – and nonsensical. I understood at an early age that there were many things that didn't make sense.

And there were things that seemed to make sense at the time and yet had no apparent genesis or logic. Do you remember anybody telling you not to walk on the cracks between paving stones? Those sorts of superstitions seem to be absorbed by osmosis when you're young. (Was hopscotch just a more sophisticated version of avoiding the cracks?) And, as I grew older, these things developed in their own way. So I would lift my feet imperceptibly to 'jump' over intersecting roads if I was upstairs on the bus. And tell fortunes to myself as I washed the dishes – whoever's cup came out last, they would live the longest, and so on.

The childish foolishness that superstition is – but perhaps because of our desire for some certainty or control of our world, it's a powerful thing that many of us never grow out of. There was even superstition in place of explanation.

One of the superstitions I grew up with was about shoes on tables. Well I suppose it is easier to say, 'It's unlucky to put shoes on the table,' than it is to explain about germs and hygiene and the risk of disease. But even if some superstitions have a semi-logical origin, it's been lost sight of, and we're left with something as illogical and unhealthy as obsessive-compulsive disorder – with the same desperate need to know we're doing the 'right' thing. And of course, if we follow the ritual, once we think things are all right because of it we continue with that little superstition each time – so the process is perpetuated and the petty obsession reinforced – *not* to do it might be risky, and besides, what harm can it do?

'The worst superstition is to consider our own tolerable'
Doris Lessing

And so we wish our little superstitions into invisibility to avoid rational thought. We need our lucky rabbit's foot to pass the exam, or get our driver's licence – but it didn't do the rabbit much good, did it?

Life is *much* more unpredictable and mysterious than the superstitious believe. (And how *do* you disentangle religion and superstition?). Superstition is like thinking you'll get wise by eating a good book.

Another ritual I had made for myself in those days was that if I flushed the toilet I had to be downstairs before the sound of the cistern filling had stopped. This was when I was very small, and I remember tripping at the top step and flying down towards the wall where the stairs turned right at the bottom. I know my father had been sitting on the settee in the living room, and how he got to me from there I don't know, but catch me he did – quite safe. Whether it stopped me running downstairs, I don't remember – maybe I just walked very quickly from then on.

There is a wise French saying: 'It's unlucky to be superstitious'

Maybe we would understand superstition better if we recognised it as an irrational by-product of our underlying desire for happiness – the word 'luck' after all, derives from 'glück', the German word for happiness.

Equally powerful is the desire to avoid unhappiness (or 'bad' luck – etymologically an oxymoron). So we imbue the unknown originators of our own superstitious inheritance with some kind of petty omniscience.

Seeing one magpie then becomes an omen of ill to come, and seeing two an omen of good.

It's all very *ominous* in the literal sense, and an indication of one thing only – woolly thinking. And the woolly thinking is sadly accumulative.

> 'Destiny does not send us heralds. She is too wise or too cruel for that.'
>
> Oscar Wilde

If we see a single magpie and something unfortunate happens (however much later), we can make a causal connection (even if the 'cause' is our own negativity) and so strengthen our naive beliefs.

> 'If you are waiting for bad luck, you will soon find it.'
>
> Japanese proverb

If we see two magpies, we may be on the lookout for, and may even create, some small happiness for ourselves.

Similarly with the commonly held belief that 'bad things happen in threes' – most things, given an indeterminate time frame, will happen in threes (or fours, or whatever).

There is too – in pursuit of the impossible (and ultimately scarily undesirable, if we thought about it!) foreknowledge and total control of our lives that superstition promises – a shadowy, lazy *pleasure* to be had from abdicating this control to unknown demiurges, and freeing ourselves from the necessity to *think*.

It's a great system for evading the responsibility for our own lives – a sort of 'But I don't want to grow up yet!' complete with mental foot stamping.

> 'It is bad luck to fall out of a 13th storey window on a Friday.'
>
> American proverb

Examined rationally, of course, new superstitions can be created at any time. If seeing the magpie can make a difference in our lives, then taking one sip of tea or two could make a difference – everything we do could make a difference. And, in the flow of things, everything *does* make a difference, and (sadly for the superstitious) therefore ends up making no difference at all.

We live our lives, they are as they are, and there are *no* predictors of our destiny – beyond the rational ones. (It is possible to predict, for example, that someone who walks into the road with his or her eyes shut may experience some *very* bad luck.)

Religion may sometimes appear to reinforce, or at least find it difficult to negate, superstition, as it may also seem to require an element of irrationality (as too may Poetry and Art and Music).

> 'No sooner had Jesus knocked over the dragon of superstition than Paul boldly set it on its legs again in the name of Jesus.'
>
> George Bernard Shaw

But how do we untwine superstition from the vast areas of our existence – our inner and our outer environment – about which we know nothing?

How can we evolve as *conscious* beings, moving forward in our thinking and our understanding and our emotional responses? How can we free ourselves from those archaic habits – the primal mud from which our *minds* have not yet emerged? And yet ... *without* losing the atavistic virtues of wonder and awe – or a sense of our own immanence, or our own potential, both as individuals and as a species?

As Jesus pointed out in relation to the supernatural – we can't make ourselves six inches taller by thinking it, or wishing it, or praying for it – yet in the *natural* world a mustard seed *can* move the equivalent of a mountain – which, surely, is miracle enough.

And why have I gone into this at such length, at the risk of boring you?

Perhaps because I share the sentiments of Victor Hugo:

> 'Superstition, bigotry and prejudice, ghosts though they are, cling tenaciously to life; they are shades armed with tooth and claw. They must be grappled with unceasingly, for it is a fateful part of human destiny that it is condemned to wage perpetual war against ghosts ...'

For Ireland has lived too long with that unholy trinity of superstition, bigotry and prejudice. And no Saint Patrick to banish them or bind them.

Anyway ...

Three

MY FATHER HAD WORKED AS A FIREFIGHTER with the American Air Force at the base near Lough Neagh during the war. He wanted to go to America after the war, but, Irish families being the way they are, the ties were too strong to break, particularly for my mother. They lost their savings when they bought an ice-cream round instead, from someone who cheated them. I suppose one disappointment after another couldn't have helped his health. God, he was still only twenty-something and had lost a lung, and his garden, and his dreams.

I was always too sensitive as a child, and I remember giving my parents problems one year when we went for our holidays to a boarding house on the north coast – Portrush, or Ballycastle perhaps.

From the moment we arrived in this poor woman's house (she seemed to be there alone), I was overwhelmed by the darkness and misery of it, and cried to leave. I was quieted and told it was all right – but when the meal was served the greens were full of dead 'earywigs', so we left anyway.

I don't know if it was the same holiday, but I remember being woken, unafraid on my mother's knee, in the front of an old Austin my father had been lent. The engine had gone on fire and smoke was seeping through under the dashboard. We stopped near a one-pump garage and shop, and, while the men dealt with the fire, I remember being fussed over by the kind woman from the shop – and the half-asleep pleasures of the lemonade and biscuits she gave us.

At some point our father bought us a car of our own, though – an old Armstrong-Siddeley that had been repainted, with a brush, in dark blue – with big stand-up chromed headlights, a rubber running-board, mahogany picnic tables for the back seats, and rope and leather handles to hang on to going round corners. Perhaps it was the similarity to an old American gangster car that had attracted him to it – though he drove it calmly and carefully, as if out of respect to the Silver Sphinx crouched on the bonnet.

We went in it to the Oul' Lammas Fair at Ballycastle, by way of the Antrim Coast Road. It poured down, and our cousin Elizabeth, who had Down's Syndrome and was not one for irony, sang 'Heavenly Sunshine'.

I can still see the streams spilling and spitting from the mountains, tumbling from the Glens – racing, peaty water that looked like cold tea. And coming down into Cushendun and Cushendall – names that are still magic to me – and the power of the sea.

It was a puzzling thing, being young with a cousin who didn't seem quite the same. No one spoke to us about it, and I wondered for a long time if *I* was the one who was different. So eventually I asked my mother, who said, 'No,' Elizabeth was the one who was a 'wee bit wanting'. But my mother used to get cross and tell me off for looking vacant, if I drifted into an absent-minded world of my own, so I still wondered if I was the odd one out.

Four

MY GRANDA ROBERTS' FATHER WAS A foundling.
He was left 'wrapped in good linen' on a doorstep in
the village of Gilford in the County Down.

I sometimes wonder if he was a bit of a changeling as well –
he had a gift for healing animals, and was known as a 'horse
doctor'. His son, my grandfather, was 68 when I was born, and
became one of my best friends in life. Granda never spoke of
his father to me, but then I never asked. Granda himself had a
profound belief in the fairies, which was untouched by his move
to smoke-blackened Belfast. He told Carole and me about the
man who scorned the fairies, and took an axe to cut down their
thorn tree. On the first blow he fell down and his arm was
paralysed. It didn't heal until the wound on the tree had healed.

Well, the man might have had a stroke, and it took as long for his arm to heal as it did for the tree to grow, but what's the difference in the end? Only in the world view.

This was Granda's way, part of how he had seen the world, since he lay at his ease in the grass watching the fairies, in the summer days of his youth in the County Armagh. He had simply seen something others hadn't, and he never made a big thing of it.

It is an interesting thought that Granda, who was born in 1880, had lived in a United Ireland – albeit one most definitely under British rule – until he was in his forties.

It was in 1921 that Partition – the political separation of the northern part of the country – was introduced. Before that time there would have been no difference in the way people thought about Newry or Sligo, Derry or Dublin, Belfast or Cork – they were all just *Irish* towns and cities. When the border was established though, and separatist political and religious movements entrenched – in a similar process to that which happens when children are educated in an exclusive and isolated way: as Protestant or Catholic, Muslim or Jew, rich or poor, black or white – differences could be accentuated and 'the other side' demonised from a solid foundation of ignorance and disassociation, both the fuel and the product of segregation and hatred.

So two countries would grow up where one had been before.

The resulting xenophobia and religious paranoia would pervert the political systems, and, in turn, be exploited by most of the politicians and leaders. Their politics did, after all, carry the genuine, if irrational, conviction that God was on *their* side.

'He that is void of wisdom despiseth his neighbour.'
Proverbs 11:12

So my grandmother and grandfather had moved from the country, some time before Partition, to 46 Electric Street – which joined Magnetic Street – part of the grid of cobbled streets that housed the mill workers of Victorian Belfast. But my grandmother had died around the time I was born, so I have no memory of her. She was spoken of as a kind woman, who had, chalked on her back door, the mysterious marks of passing tramps, to whom she would give bread and butter, and a few coppers. She was told that one tramp was seen throwing away the bread, as he went to spend the money in Dan's Bar, but it made no dent in her generosity.

Ah, Dan's Bar – what a smell and a roar from inside, as the etched glass doors on the corner swung open as you walked past on the pavement, holding on to a grown-up's hand. A sweet and sickly smell, hard to describe, inseparable from the noise. A heavy fug of gaslit smoking and drinking. To a child it was both warm and sinister. A powerful scent that I've never come across since – a lost smell from another era.

My grandparents didn't drink – I suppose they came through the time of Gin and Temperance, and 'drunk for a ha'penny, dead drunk for a penny'. (And I suppose they could have added, 'dead for a penny ha'penny'.)

Dan's Bar stood on a corner by the bridge on Roden Street. On the other side of the bridge was the City Mission Hall – a building that in the uncertainty of memory looks like it should have been made from corrugated iron, but was probably bleak red brick.

Under the bridge between the bar and the Mission Hall flowed – or slithered – the aptly named River Blacky. The only life in the River Blacky took the form of leeches.

Though it was a shallow river, and a short bridge, the gap between Dan's Bar and the City Mission might as well have been filled by the River Styx for the contrast between them. Though on which bank was Life, and on which Death, I still don't know.

I was never inside Dan's Bar, but I was taken from the refuge of my Granda's house every Sunday evening either to the City Mission, or Saint Philip's Church on the Grosvenor Road. Granda himself never came with us. His was a freer spirit. The only thing I ever knew of Granda's religious opinions, was that – as far as he was concerned – Jesus was a Socialist.

The City Mission had a legend painted on the far wall: WORSHIP THE LORD IN THE BEAUTY OF HOLINESS and they might as well have added, 'because that's the only beauty you'll get around here'.

Well aye, it's all under the concrete of the Westlink now.

On down Roden Street was the house where Auntie Annie and Uncle John lived. They had been to New York. Auntie Annie said when they moved to their first apartment there, and she looked out of the window, she thought she was looking down at black beetles and ants, before she realised they were cars and people.

Uncle John knew about Speakeasies and Prohibition, but

apart from Auntie Annie saying 'erbs' and not 'herbs', America seemed not to have changed them at all.

The scullery in their house smelt of fresh watercress and strong cheese, and we would sit and eat in the 'working kitchen' at the table with its oilcloth cover, by the window looking out to the yard.

When I was very small, Uncle John laughingly told me he would 'hang me up by the lugs from the washing line' and I burst into tears, not because I thought he was serious, but because I must have done something wrong without meaning to. And then I'm crying because I'm ashamed of myself for crying.

There is something wonderful too from that time. I'm sitting on the bare wood of their top stairs, by the attic. The window facing me has deep red and blue glass strips around it, with etched stars in the corners. I'm reading a copy of *Kidnapped* – four illustrations to a yellowing page, and the full text at the bottom. The dusty, faintly wood and celery scent of that book has stayed with me for life. Very, very occasionally I come across that smell, that essence that summons up all that I love about books. And I am five or six years old again, transported back to where I was first taken to a different place, led to another world, by a book.

They gave me that favourite old volume of Robert Louis Stevenson's, and it is one of life's losses that it has disappeared. And it is one of life's treasures when I catch its smell, fleetingly, somewhere, and am reminded.

In the attic too, was a game of bagatelle, painted a dusty

green. The sound the pins made, as the steel ball fired from the spring struck them, was more a part of the pleasure of the game than the score you got.

There too was an old, beautifully made, air rifle, which no longer worked but was still a very desirable object for a boy. I was given it later, and overcame its deficiencies by making the noises with my mouth that only small boys think sound like gunfire.

In their front parlour Auntie Annie and Uncle John kept a set of old encyclopaedias. On a Sunday, when we visited them, I could sit on the floor looking at cutaway engravings of Dreadnoughts, under the big bright framed print of Turner's 'Fighting Temeraire' on the chimney breast, above the pair of brass cobra candlesticks on the mantelpiece. Auntie Annie was fond of the salerooms and, if she had slightly eccentric tastes, had a more interesting house as a result.

Those pictures from my early life form an eclectic group, with nothing more obvious to connect them than that they remain in my memory.

From that print of Turner's 'Fighting Temeraire' and those evocative illustrations in *Kidnapped*, they form a downward graph, to bump at the bottom into a black and white photograph, from a Sunday school prize book, of a robin nesting in an old kettle. I remember leaning on the windowsill of my bedroom on a quiet, summer day and looking at that photograph – a silent message from a world I wished I lived in, for some indecipherable reason. Perhaps I wanted to live in a world that thinks a robin in an old kettle is important.

There too, for no particular reason, is Joseph and his coloured coat in Auntie Sally's old illustrated Bible.

And the framed prints of idyllic cottage gardens, with Biblical texts across cloudless blue skies (though I can't remember the moral, only the flowers – a lot of lupins and delphiniums). Carole and I regularly won these at Sunday School for being able to recite verses from the Bible – which we did with all the identification with the text and the nuance of delivery of a pair of parrots.

There is the cover of *Steamboat Bill*, whose boat blew up in a race, illustrated brilliantly, with a deep hallucinogenic glow of blues and autumn golds – the lifebelt around his head, like a parody of the sailor on the Player's Navy Cut cigarette packets.

Here the endpapers of the Rupert Bear annuals, those receding wooded mists that I took myself for a walk through, and could get lost in.

A reverie, a daydream – the picture as catalyst, as poetry, as an initiator of unpredictable processes and musings.

Here is the girl I fell in love with, from a dark book of fairy tales in black and white, probably drawn by Arthur Rackham – I recall that it was a large book with a green cloth cover, and poor quality thick paper.

She has beautiful eyes, an air of sadness – and such big but graceful feet!

And sometimes, from an unexpected source, something small and anonymous could make a lasting impression.

Like those silent blue skies in my Roy Rogers annual.

As a small boy those skies affected me with their quiet power – I would look at them for ages. Although I could not have articulated it then, and at the risk of sounding silly, they seemed to hold the same openness, the same possibility, the same sense of the Infinite that I would find in William Blake's work many, many years later.

I would hazard a guess that the person who painted those strange blue skies had enjoyed them, and wondered about them, as much as I.

Nowadays they remind me too of something further in my past, when my father would sing me to sleep with:

> Home, home on the range
> Where the deer and the antelope play;
> Where seldom is heard a discouraging word,
> And the skies are not cloudy all day.

He was not blessed with what you could call a fine singing voice, but it was still so pleasant and comforting that I would open my eyes straightaway if he tried to stop.

There is only one actual photograph that sits in the same part of my mind as these other pictures. It is a slightly fuzzy vignette of a young man in naval uniform. He has an expression both open and smiling, yet at the same time withheld and reserved.

This was my uncle, my father's brother, George Golding Gepp, who was a 'medic' and had died after a torpedo attack in the war.

My father had framed his image with bevelled glass, between two brass pillars – which were large rounds of B17 ammunition pointing skywards – on a perspex base. It sat in the alcove by the fireplace in Granda Gepp's parlour in Euterpe Street.

On the wall by the yard window, in the sitting room behind, hung a print of a lone grey corvette, seen from in front, moving through a swell under the subtle coloured clouds of a dawn sky.

My father's dream would have been to command that solitary corvette but his older brother was the only one allowed to go to sea, or war. George was the tearaway to my father's steady hand. He had been sent to Australia for a while to try to change his gambling habits. He had fathered a child by a girlfriend in Scotland (whom I think Auntie Ivy visited quietly in later years). Then he got all respectable and then he was killed.

Auntie Ivy gave me his signet ring when I was older. It was reddish gold with three intertwined Gs engraved in copperplate script. I wore it for some time, until once, on my way back to college, dozing on the steamer to Heysham, the smell of diesel and a heavy sea made me dream of him, and the chaos in which he met his end.

I threw the ring into the Irish Sea from a beach near where we landed. It seemed a fitting thing to do, and a small gesture of respect – even from the rebellious and arrogantly anti-military young man I had become.

Ah, that corvette. It still rides a lonely sea and a dawn sky in my mind. And I think of my father, and of my uncle whom I never knew, and that last mysterious voyage on which we all depart, and I wish them well.

I think of Mendelssohn's overture, 'Calm Sea and Prosperous Voyage', and its origin in those two poems of Goethe (which date from a time when a calm sea could be as troubling to the sailor's mind as a storm):

Silence deep rules o'er the waters,	Tiefe Stille herrscht im Wasser
Calmly slumbering lies the main,	Ohne Regung ruht das Meer,
While the sailor views with trouble	Und bekümmert sieht der Schiffer
Nought but one vast level plain.	Glatte Fläche rings umher.
Not a zephyr is in motion!	Keine Luft von Keiner Seite!
Silence fearful as the grave!	Todesstille fürchterlich!
In the mighty waste of ocean	In der ungeheuren Weite
Sunk to rest is ev'ry wave.	Reget keine Welle sich.

– *Calm at Sea* 1795

The mist is fast clearing	Die Nebel zerreißen,
And radiant is heaven,	Der Himmel ist helle,
Whilst Aeolus loosens	Und Aeolus löset
Our anguish-fraught bond.	Das ängstliche Band.

| The zephyrs are sighing, | Es säuseln die Winde, |
| Alert is the sailor. | Es rührt sich der Schiffer. |

Quick! Nimbly be plying!	Geschwinde! Geschwinde!
The billows are riven,	Es teilt sich die Welle,
The distance approaches;	Es naht sich die Ferne,
I see land beyond!	Schon seh' ich das Land!

–The Prosperous Voyage 1795

And I listen and think how the wind 'loosens our anguish-fraught bond' and allows us to make sail for the next future: 'The distance approaches; I see land beyond'.

My Granda Roberts' house around the corner in Electric Street was much more sparse and simple than either Auntie Annie's or Granda Gepp's. To me it was more homely than either. Granda sat in a big upright wooden chair without cushions, and would doze there for a while after his lunch.

The only touch of comfort was a green leatherette chaise longue that sat in the alcove to the right of the fireplace. The rest of the chairs were simple bentwood things with pierced plywood seats. Granda had made a stool for us children to sit on. He loved carpentry, and later built a shed in the yard for his workbench and tools, where he would allow me to footer about too. The stool was oak, of a simple, sturdy structure – two end panels with inverted Vs cut in the bottom, two shallow sides to brace it, and a top. The top had a diamond shape cut in it for picking it up.

On Granda's mantelpiece sat an electric clock, a small carved bog oak cauldron, and an enamelled brass 'Auxiliary Fire Service' matchbox holder. In the hearth was a cylinder of wooden 'spills' for lighting the gas stove in the kitchen, or a pipe or cigarettes from the fire – though Granda hadn't smoked his pipe in years. On the walls were two small oil paintings, by my Uncle James. One was of a pine forest in Canada where he had lived with his wife – my Aunt Lily and Granda's second daughter – for a while. The other was of an Irish cottage with a woman feeding the hens. For one reason or another I loved that picture. The only other thing on the wall was a calendar in the shape of a shamrock.

There was a table with an oilcloth cover under the window to the street, and a half-glazed door with panes of patterned glass, that led to the small tiled hallway. The hall was just big enough for the front door (always open in good weather) to swing into.

Granda's house was lit, when daylight faded, by a glaring electric light in the middle of the ceiling. His next-door neighbour, Edi Cochrane, a small, self-effacing wee woman, had kept hers gaslit. I was only in there once or twice, but I remember the unexpected bright yellowness of it. After the candles and oil lamps of the previous century, it seemed that quantity rather than quality of light was what was wanted.

Granda had always moved with the times. Later he was the first person in the family to buy a television. It was a deep rounded, veneered thing, with a catch on top you pushed so that a trapdoor sprang open to let you move the dials – though there was only one station: the BBC. Like the wireless, the television took a long time to warm up. It lived on a shelf halfway up the wall to the left of the fireplace.

Upstairs, Granda had a complete set of Dickens that had been bought in instalments.

On his bedroom mantelpiece there was a cowrie shell that we put to our ears and listened to the sea.

My parents were living with Granda when I was born, but I only remember the house from later, when I used to go and see him. Then at lunchtime we would have cups of tea, and soda bread with bananas or Tate and Lyle's Golden Syrup ('Out of the Strong came forth Sweetness'). And when he cut the bread he would take the board outside and dust the crumbs off with his cloth cap, onto the cobbles for the pigeons. If your parents were there you would have to say Grace before you ate, and we would rattle through:

> Thank you for the world so sweet
> Thank you for the food we eat
> Thank you for the birds that sing
> Thank you God for everything. Amen.

in five seconds. (Except when Elizabeth said it – she had a stammer and it took longer, so Carole or I would always volunteer.)

In the afternoon maybe you'd have some ginger snaps or Jacob's Fig Rolls washed down with sarsaparilla, or one of the other 'Minerals' that were kept in the cool under the stone sink in the scullery. I was allowed to drink from his big green porcelain mug, with a picture of a jaunting car on the side, and would emerge after every few gulps, with grateful gasps.

(I remember, too, the smell of Pears soap on Granda's cheek as we kissed him goodbye after each visit.)

If we stayed for tea at Granda's it was generally fish and chip from Liegghio's – which we pronounced 'Leekeeoh's' (or sometimes, in what we thought was a witty reference to their home-made ice-cream, 'Lick–eeoh's'.) Their shop was around the corner, at the other end of Electric Street from Dan's Bar. You were served by 'Wee Benny' who had a congenital limp and was very small and cheerful. Several members of his family had been interned in the Second World War, probably as 'enemy aliens', but rumour had it that they'd been taken away because the old man couldn't bring himself to use powdered milk in his ice-cream – as he was supposed to by wartime regulations – so bought real milk on the black market instead. The story may not have made their fortune, but it ensured that when they were released they were local heroes – and their ice-cream was great.

On a gable end near Liegghio's was a picture of King Billy, unusual in being a head and shoulders portrait and not the traditional (mounted on a white horse treading over dead Jacobites on the banks of the Boyne) version. It would be a full half century before I would find out that, in fact, King Billy's horse had got stuck in the mud on the further banks of the Boyne, King Billy had an asthma attack, and was carted off to safety by a big fellow from Enniskillen: as for poor King James, he was so frightened he stayed a few miles down the road, away from the battle altogether. The facts put a more human face to that divisive and iconic event, don't they?

From almost anywhere in Belfast you can see mountains – that was true then as now. But I can remember walking up the Grosvenor Road towards my grandfather's house with the Black Mountain at an untouchable and hazy distance: it may as well have been in another country. Sheets of newspaper blew about and dust cut your eyes. The old shawlies who lived down the side streets were keeping their black, fringed wraps tightly round their bent heads and the babies they wet-nursed, as they went about their – to my childish mind, mysterious – lives.

Granda was a great walker, but it was Auntie Annie who first took us away from the dusty city and up to the Black Mountain, and on to the peat bog that swayed beneath our feet – collecting stray bits of lambs' wool on the way as a cure for the earache.

I remember a blue and white sky, and bouncing up and down on the grey and green clouds of mosses and lichens. Auntie Annie was very religious, and for me there is still something of the true nature of Heaven in this memory of her.

On the south-eastern side of that mountain, by a track called the Mountain Loney, is a spring that has gushed from a hole in the rock there, since ancestral times and before – ice cold water from the heart of the mountain – a holy well, but only in the sense that it gave its water freely to the children, of any religion or none, who were drawn to it from all over the city, some pushing their bicycles or carrying smaller children. Unremarked and uncontaminated by religious or commercial concerns, it was just *there*, and how we loved it. We would quench our thirst to the full, and then fill our empty lemonade bottles or plastic canteens with its freezing waters.

For me, that spring up the Mountain Loney provides the most poignant and melancholy metaphor of the troubled time that followed. In the 1970s, after the killing had started, I returned there (looking for the best of my childhood, I suppose) and found that someone had drilled holes in the rock and bolted a rusty pipe to take all of the water for themselves.

It seemed then that in all of that part of Ireland, instead of the pure, cold water of my childhood, blood had begun to flow – like some perverse and evil inversion of the Christian rites, that were now themselves warped and hijacked as completely as they were in the Crusades, to the cause of murder and hatred.

William Blake wrote that 'War is Energy enslaved'; and for me that rusty pipe symbolised the damming over time of the potential for good, and its transmutation into the divisive and destructive force that exploded through the body of that mouldering Victorian city, and bloodied forever the lives of those who lived there.

It was Auntie Annie also who told me, many years later, that two men had called at Electric Street when she was a young girl, and gone into the back room with my Granda. They'd offered him money from the family of his father, the foundling. She said she saw the box with sovereigns piled high in it. But

Granda told them that if they hadn't cared up to now, they needn't bother. And they and the box were sent on their way. Anyway, neither the men nor the magic box were ever seen again, and if they had returned I think Granda would have told them much the same. For he always seemed to me like a man who had as much as he wanted. He kept his pride – and he had coals in the hearth and food on the table.

At some point Granda decided we'd all go to the Free State for a holiday. We stayed at Greystones near Bray, to the south of Dublin, and I can remember little of the details or where we stayed or anything – just a sheltered beach, lapping gentle waves – not even big enough to make foam – and I'm swimming – I can swim! And I'm bobbed up and down and get a mouthful of the sea trying to shout for them to look at me, but it doesn't put me off – *me*, who would burst into tears of shame and frustration if my swimming sister splashed water at me, *I could swim*, and that deep delight is beyond description. So Greystones (which few have ever heard of) is always special to me, for that one great thing. I must go back some time and look, and maybe, maybe, even swim there again. (Though as more of the whale than the waif these days: Granda always said that if a man put on weight around the middle in his forties, as he had, he wouldn't get rid of it again. As I get older I get more like him in so many ways.)

Five

THERE IS ANOTHER PICTURE IN MY mind, only remembered by being remembered. A slab of blue sky, reddish brick of houses, cobbled grey of road. A dry and dusty image, *my earliest memory* – a place without trees, without trace of greenery. It has the strange motionless silence of a de Chirico painting – a powerful unnaturalness. This is a part of the Belfast I was born into. This is what I saw from my pram. And sometimes my mother moves into the frame of the pram hood – a yellow and rust, belted tweed overcoat and a brown 1950s dinner-plate hat. This must have been 'Broadway', where my parents moved to live after Electric Street. Both streets had no gardens, no trees – an environment that didn't even feel *man*-made. So total was the absence of nature you felt that it had always been this way, would always be this way and it could no more be changed than could the geology. And yet the spirit knows the lack of beauty, and bemoans it, or becomes twisted by it. This was Belfast – these were the sorts of streets most people lived in. And on the main roads and in the city centre the electric wires of trams and trolleybuses netted even the sky – there was still less room for the spirit to soar. Is it any wonder the place would split apart? On the tectonic plates of ignorance and fear.

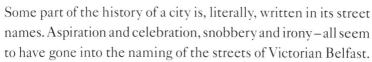

Some part of the history of a city is, literally, written in its street names. Aspiration and celebration, snobbery and irony – all seem to have gone into the naming of the streets of Victorian Belfast.

Some were straightforward and basic: Steam Mill Lane, Workman Road, Factory Street; Hemp and Flax and Linenhall streets. Some, like Electric and Magnetic streets, seem an eccentric celebration of science, industry and technology – there was also Ampere Street; Chemical, Crystal, Mica and Mineral streets – and Chlorine Gardens. Then there were those that commemorated the history of an empire – named for Agincourt, Trafalgar and Waterloo; Riley, Jellicoe and Kitchener streets; Crimea, Albert and Victoria. And there were those that tried to redefine the city as an extended part of the Home Counties –

Kensington Gardens, Oxford Street, Shaftesbury Avenue, Dorchester Drive; Dover, Windsor, Wimbledon and Westminster streets; Suffolk, Sussex, Sydenham, Surrey.

The religious tradition was noted in the area known as 'The Holy Land' near the university – with streets called Carmel and Palestine, Jerusalem, Damascus and Cairo.

Others seem to have been named with irony, for who could call these brick terraces, built in the gloom of the factory chimney, with outside lavatories and no bathrooms, after Thalia and Euterpe, the Greek muses of poetry and music? And what strange sensibility should name Pandora Street after the bringer of the ills of the world and the imprisoner of Hope?

When we went to visit my other grandfather who lived in Euterpe Street, or our Auntie Ivy, his daughter who lived with him, we would catch the red bus from Finaghy to Bradbury Place, and walk round past 'Mosie Hunter's', the big pub on the corner, to the bus stop on the Donegall Road. We waited for the bus next to the screaming rip and noise and tangy smell of the sawmill that opened onto the pavement.

The coalman with his horse and cart and blackened sacks of coal would go up the road. And sometimes the coalbrick man, with his coalbricks on a flat cart, the bricks still steaming from the factory and matching the breath from his horse on a cold day. A coalbrick cart came up our street in Finaghy too – the driver's street cry just recognisable, 'Coaall–BRXX! Coaall–BRXX!'

Coalbricks were made from coal dust. They were cheap and glowed red in the fire and gave out little heat compared to coal. They were the mark and relief of real poverty. When people weren't so poor and anyone showed any minor extravagance, like buying a new hat or something, they would be teased with the cry of, 'No poverty here – throw on another coalbrick!'

My Granda Gepp's parents had left Ireland and moved with the British army in India to Bangalore, where Granda was born in the 1880s in the 'European Females Hospital' – which says it all, I suppose.

His family returned to Ireland and I sometimes think the child never recovered from moving to this dark northern city. Away from sunshine, and real oranges, and clean air, and servants, I expect.

I can only remember him as an old man. He would take me to go and play on the rusting roundabouts and swings in the bleak, squeaking 'playground' across the Donegall Road. Afterwards he would lift me up to see over the vertical sleepers that made the walls of the footbridge over the railway, so I could see the trains run underneath, hear them shaking and snorting, smell the steam coal.

In the 1950s the railway ran under the Donegall Road into the main station in Great Victoria Street through huge soot-smeared cuttings. If you came into the city by train, on the right, in massive sans serif letters in once white glazed tiles, on a wall of blackened brick, was the phrase GOD IS LOVE. It didn't evoke love: on the contrary, to a child, its size and appearance were chilling. It held a sense of damnation and exclusion, of the threat of a hell beyond the one in which it seemed already placed (and another, bloodier, which would manifest itself before long).

Euterpe Street was still lit by gas lamps then. The lamplighter came round at dusk, with some sort of long pole he used, to open the lamps and light them.

In the dry, limewashed attic of my grandfather's house there was an ancient copy of *Pilgrim's Progress*, two long triangular bayonets with brass and leather cases, a leather bandolier and a silver-topped 'swagger stick' – all bits and pieces from his father's time in India, I suppose. There was also a toy speedboat – or torpedo boat – hull, beautifully constructed of plywood, and almost three foot long, that my father or his brother must have started to build and abandoned at some point.

Granda Gepp had a trick with a ha'penny, where he rubbed it on his knee until it disappeared (it slid down to his trouser turn-up). He taught us riddles: 'What goes up the chimney down, but won't come down the chimney up?' (an umbrella) and religious words (which I've forgotten) to the tune of the Westminster Chimes on the clock in his living room.

In the front parlour was the piano with its candleholders, on which all I ever learned to play was 'Chopsticks' or 'Can you wash your Daddy's shirt?/Can you make it clean?/Can you wash your Daddy's shirt and bleach it on the green?'

And the big stone fire-surround with the gas fire with its round pebbles instead of coals, which made a frightening loud pop when it was lit. Next to the fireplace was a bookshelf with the *Newnes' Pictorial Knowledge*, in seven volumes – a sort of children's encyclopaedia, with its real treasure being the pictures 'Specially drawn for this work', especially the folding paper models at the back. These were like exploded drawings: as you carefully turned back layer after paper layer they would reveal more detail – of the biplane airliner, the queen bee and drone, the apple, the rose or the green water frog.

So Granda Gepp had tried his best for us, but his mind had been stressed by too much religion and loss. His wife had died. His eldest son had been killed.

When I was six or seven I remember being looked after in his house by my Auntie Ivy.

I was sitting on a chair reading the *Beano* or *Dandy* when he returned. My aunt grabbed the comics from me before he came in and pushed them under the seat cushion, telling me that Granda didn't like comics. I couldn't quite grasp this notion, so, to test it, when he came into the room I pulled out the comics and started reading. He went mad – not at me, but at Auntie Ivy; comics were the Work of the Devil, she knew they weren't to be brought into the house, and on and on – as if the *Beano* and the *Dandy* were responsible for the Sins of the World.

The Seven 'Deadly' Sins, after all, are: Pride, Covetousness, Lust, Envy, Gluttony, Anger, Sloth - and I don't think the *Beano* or the *Dandy* or any of the other comics we read promoted any of those; quite the opposite, in fact.

St Gregory the Great, in sixth century Rome, had decided these seven were 'deadly' because they in turn caused other sins.

On that basis the good saint should surely have included the Humiliation of Others as the eighth (though maybe he saw it as a sub-division of the first, Pride).

Humiliation is the real snake among social sins – it stings deeply and comes back even more venomously to bite another innocent soul. The only way the infection doesn't spread is if the person bitten is saintly enough not to respond, and strong enough not to let it fester. Auntie Ivy should have been canonised many times over.

Granda Gepp, as a fundamentalist, wouldn't have had any time for the notion of Deadly Sins anyway, whatever their number – he would have considered that as part of the theology of Rome.

Memories are long in Ireland, but thoroughly selective, and in most cases predicated on the political/cultural/religious standpoint of the person – which too often hasn't changed since the accident of birth burdened them with one bag or the other. And the Irish are *all* good at not letting facts stand in the way of a good (hi)story.

Granda Gepp would have been outraged if he had been told that we were all Catholics once. And furious if he had been told that if you defame that faith, you are, in effect, insulting the long line of your own ancestors, who were also – uncomfortable thought – pagans before that again (whatever a 'pagan' was – probably someone with a good deal more country sense and compassion than many of the 'Christians' in Ireland). You could have aroused his fury even more directly – to the point of apoplexy I should think – by bluntly pointing out that he wouldn't be here if it hadn't been for Catholics having sex. But I was never old enough to light any of those fuses – or engage in an enlightened discussion about any of these issues – whichever.

My Granda the Ayatollah; his Grandson the Heretic. And comics weren't the only things he hated: the cinema would have been on the proscribed list too. And probably most books except the Bible, *Pilgrim's Progress* and *Newnes' Pictorial Knowledge*. As for Drinking and Dancing, it went without saying. Television hadn't arrived yet, and I don't know what his opinion was about the wireless – I don't remember there being one in the house though.

Sadly, he wasn't alone in his extremism – 'Ulster Sundays'

were famous for their miserableness; though, if you were a Catholic child, you were at least allowed to play after Mass.

I remember being with some other children near the Crossroads in Finaghy, and an old man, black hat, Bible in hand, said to us, 'What are you boys doing, *laughing* on the Sabbath?' I can remember going red with embarrassment, as though I'd done something desperately wrong.

After the fuss about The Comics, my mother stood up to Granda Gepp and told him we were her and Sam's children, and she would bring us up as she saw fit, and if that involved the cinema and comics, well that was up to them, and not him.

She always said afterwards that she thought he respected her more for that – though she was a nervous woman, so it must have taken real courage on her part. He was a formidable man, and must have scared the Hell out of people, or more accurately, into them, when he went around the countryside preaching, which he did occasionally.

In the callous and careless way of children, I didn't really like or understand Granda Gepp much after this.

It was about three or four years later, when I was nine or ten, that my mother came up to our bedrooms to tell us he had died, and I remember saying, 'Does that mean we don't have to go to school today?'

But Granda Gepp must have been much 'respected', because I remember being taken to watch the funeral procession on the Donegall Road, which was lined thick with people, as he was carried out of Euterpe Street and up the road to God knows where.

(As I grew older – it's a hard thing to say – but I generally thought of my Granda Gepp with scorn, if I thought of him at all. That feeling remained until I was about eighteen or twenty. Then halfway between waking and sleeping one night, I had a picture of him in my mind's eye, with the tears running down his face – he wasn't looking at me. And I realised that was what I hadn't seen – the pain he was in, and the tears he had shed.)

And isn't it strangely appropriate, that half a century on, and pondering these things, I should, just this sunny morning, in papers that are quite unconnected, come across a solitary quote from Pilgrim's Progress?

> Poor man! Where art thou now? Thy day is night
> Good man, be not cast down, thou yet art right,
> Thy way to Heaven lies by the gates of Hell;
> Cheer up, hold out, with thee it shall go well.

In those days (the 1950s) my father wore a black armband sewn on his overcoat for a certain length of time, which was then replaced by a hatchment – a black diamond shape – for another length of time – indicators of degrees of mourning. Why and when did that custom just vanish?

As Marcus Aurelius says: 'Light and dark, dark and light – all lives are made like this – and envy is ignorance.'

Six

And [Jesus] took a child and set him in the midst of them:

And when he had taken him in his arms, he said unto them, 'Whosoever shall receive one of such children in my name receiveth me ... And whosoever shall offend one of these little ones that believe in me, it is better for him that a millstone were hanged about his neck, and he were cast into the sea.'

–The Gospel according to St Mark, Chapter 9

MY MOTHER AND FATHER HAD HAD religion impressed on them since childhood (as had almost everyone in Ireland, North and South) so I suppose they were easily influenced to send Carole and me to Sunday School. It was probably at the urging of Granda Gepp, as it was a fundamentalist Sunday School in a Gospel Hall.

However, apart from going to church on Sunday, and teaching us to say the Grace before meals and our prayers before bed, neither my mother nor father were religious in any way that you would have noticed: they didn't talk about religion, and they weren't in the least stern or bigoted. But I suppose Carole and I going to Sunday School kept family politics calm and also allowed my parents (along with thousands of others in Northern Ireland) to have their so-called 'rest in bed' on Sunday afternoons!

For Carole it seemed of no importance one way or the other. But Sunday School, and Mission Hall, and Church were equal parts of a disastrous psychological and philosophical struggle for me. Their whole basis seemed to me, as a child, to be about Fear (though they would probably have claimed to be spreading the *love* of God). They carried the awful certainty of *knowing* they were right. And to convince others they spread the germs of Fear – of the Lord: of Death: of Sin – everywhere. They seemed obsessed by death and punishment:

'Would your soul go to Jesus if you got knocked down by a bus or a tram or a car this afternoon? Or would you be cast into eternal darkness – where the Good Book tells us there will be Weeping and Wailing and Gnashing of Teeth?!' (This delivered in a whining shriek, or the ranting phlegm of some sort of *ur*Paisley; 'gnashing of teeth' was a particularly useful phrase as people were unsettled by the fact that nobody really knew what it meant.)

And they were obsessed too by Sacrificial Lambs. And Blood. And Torture on a Cross. And Guilt – particularly *your* Guilt; they had been forgiven after all, and were assured of *their* place in Paradise.

I was repelled and revolted by it – by the sheer brainwashing power and ugliness of it all. In reaction – in my childish frustration and powerlessness – at times I felt revolted by these people too, in their rightness, and their stiffness, and their mothballed smelliness.

But there was no way out – I was supposed to believe all of this – and I tried very hard to believe it. The effort made me sick – quite literally. I sometimes had to be taken from church or Mission Hall in the middle of the evening service, for fear of throwing up, and go to the sanity of my Granda Roberts' house.

It wasn't as if these were horrible people who were forever trying to frighten children, just that their whole 'mission' was to 'make sinners repent' and so on – and for that they seemed to need Fear.

Their message seemed a *negation* of life – an eagerness for death and Paradise instead. Where it wasn't totally negative, it was couched in the strange desert imagery of the Middle East – with its Zions and Jehovahs, its Salems and Mount Sinais, its Jerusalems and Shilohs – transplanted on to a cold, dirty, sooty old Belfast (transposed quite literally, in the street names of 'The Holy Land').

Then there was the Heaven that you didn't understand and didn't really want to go to – especially if it was built on all the blood-drenched stuff they unconsciously delighted in on earth – and especially if *they* were all going to be there too!

> Little children will be there,
> Who have sought the Lord by prayer,
> From every Sunday School:
> Teachers, too, shall meet above,
> And our pastors, whom we love ...
>
> Hymn 616
> Church of Ireland Hymnal c.1955

It wasn't unrelievedly grim, of course – in church there was the genuine resonant poetry of the Psalms and some of the old Celtic hymns and Christmas carols. And individual ministers and pastors, and their wives, were often kindly souls, who genuinely meant well.

In some kind of compensation for the general lack of beauty, though, I daydreamed about building a cathedral in the built-in wardrobe of my bedroom. In reality it was full of the clutter of old toys and boxes, but in my mind's eye it became a peaceful and a holy place, with candles and stained glass windows and a vaulted ceiling. I do not know where these images came from, but I was never bothered by the practicalities – somehow I would have a cathedral in my bedroom cupboard and go there when the ugliness became too much.

But, apart from the slight thaw in the prevailing Puritanism each Christmastime, in the real world there remained an 'evangelical' – which *should* mean 'from the angels' – grimness, which owed little to angels, and had more in common with the zealotry and orthodoxy of a Saint Paul than the liberating theology of a Jesus.

And beyond that the *language* pointed, not to the heavens, but to a dark blood-thirst, a pseudo-cannibalism of flesh-eating and blood-drinking. The litany was one of torture and suffering, war waging and death, fear and guilt:

> Gives His guests His Blood for wine,
> Gives His Body for the feast;
> Christ the Victim, Christ the Priest.
>
> Hymn 145

> Bread of Heaven, on Thee we feed,
> For Thy Flesh is meat indeed.
>
> Hymn 208

> Over some foul dark spot,
> One only stream, a stream of blood,
> Can wash away the blot.
>
> Hymn 586

> There is a fountain filled with Blood,
> Drawn from Emmanuel's veins,
> And sinners plunged beneath that flood
> Lose all their guilty stains.
>
> Hymn 543

I didn't know then that this sort of imagery derived from the likes of the *taurobolium* – the bull sacrifice which had been practised in the Mediterranean area, in the early centuries of the Christian era, by the pagan cult of the Great Mother of the

Gods – when a person offering the sacrifice stood in a pit and the bull on a grid above was slaughtered, so that the participant was drenched in the gallons of blood pouring through. (The priests of the same cult would slash themselves to soak the altar and a symbolic tree with their own blood, a practice not so very different from that of the mediæval flagellants.)

I was a child – I did not know that there was a history and development of ideas within Christianity as elsewhere – it was just supposed to be 'the One True Faith' as you were given it – unchanging, eternal.

But of course, since the emperors Constantine and Theodosius and Justinian, Christianity had been an imperial force, and had adjusted to, and absorbed and adapted (or conquered) many differing customs and theologies in its onward march – and been corrupted in turn. At the stage at which I was thrown into it, it was certainly a *dualistic* theology (but without the sophistication of the old 'heresy' of Manichæism):

> Principalities and powers,
> Mustering their unseen array,
> Wait for thy unguarded hours;
> Gird thy heavenly armour on,
> Wear it ever, night and day;
> Near thee lurks the evil one ...
>
> Hymn 511

So – quite unconsciously – the Devil was as much revered as his opposite, God.

And the old man with the Bible who had told us off for

'laughing on the Sabbath' was only echoing the words of the Hymnal in the section OF PENITENCE (CHILDREN):

> All our sinful words and ways..
> All the mischief we have wrought
> All forbidden things we sought,
> All the sins to others taught..
> All our sloth and vanity,
> All our sinful levity ...
> Hymn 656

Even C.F. Alexander, the wife of the (Church of Ireland) Bishop of Derry in the mid-1800s, and the author of the famous hymn, 'There is a Green Hill Far Away', expresses similar sentiments (in Hymn 607 in the section FOR THE YOUNG):

> There's a wicked spirit
> Watching round you still,
> And he tries to tempt you
> To all harm and ill ...
> For ye promised truly
> In your infant days
> To renounce him wholly
> And forsake his ways...
> Ye must learn to fight
> With the bad within you.

– which echoes too, to the doctrine of Original Sin – that children are born, not new, pure and innocent, but as plague carriers of innate wickedness.

What a sad and impoverished philosophy people had created to punish themselves. In a polarised world of good and evil, God and Devil, it was as if they had made a division between the flower and the soil. They worshipped the flower, while damning the earth it grew from. And even then it seems the flower wasn't a lily, or a rose, but one of those creepy flesh-eating things.

I remember reading about Elijah and the prophets of Baal. The prophets of Baal had failed (in a test that Elijah proposed) to get *their* god to make their sacrificial pyre burst into flames. But Elijah prayed, and, despite *his* pyre being soaked with water three times, '... the fire of the Lord fell, and consumed the burnt sacrifice, and the wood, and the stones, and the dust, and licked up the water that was in the trench' and Elijah told the people to take the prophets of Baal (all four hundred and fifty of them) and he '... brought them down to the brook Kishon, and slew them there'.

And I could not get rid of the thought, though I struggled with it night after night in my childish mind, the *doubt* that it was not a miracle, but a cruel trick with turpentine or something – '... and licked up the water that was in the trench'.

I find it hard now to remember how heretical, how sinful this doubt seemed to me, and how I couldn't rid myself of it.

I thought I was struggling with a demon of doubt, when I was wrestling with the angel of rational thought.

'Any system of religion that has anything in it that shocks the mind of a child cannot be a true system.'

Thomas Paine [1737-1809] *The Age of Reason*

Our father always came up at night to tuck us in our beds and kiss us goodnight. Eventually I couldn't stand my lonely struggle any more, and confessed to him that I thought a 'miracle' in the Bible might be a simple magician's trick.

I can't remember what he said. It was probably as simple as, 'Aw now, don't worry about it! Think about your holidays in the Isle of Man instead.' And I was young enough still to know that he was always right – and I didn't worry about it any more.

And so I started to learn to think, and realised there were some hard thoughts to be thought. One was the notion of Jesus, that most compassionate of men, as a 'Good Shepherd'. How can there be a 'good' shepherd? He may protect the sheep from the wolves or the bears, but only so that he or his family and friends can eat them later. That didn't sound like the teachings of the Jesus I admire. And so in time I came to think of it as just another example of religious woolly thinking. And today – the joke aside – I can say that, and it takes little courage, because I know it's unlikely that I'll be vilified or martyred for it – but in the time of Elijah I would have been another burnt offering.

And, in the time to come in this part of Ireland, many would die from just such a result of people's certainty of their own rightness.

Nothing can keep people further from God than religion and certitude.

As Rabindranath Tagore says, 'Bigotry tries to keep truth safe in its hands with a grip that kills it.'

And as Lucretius says, of Agamemnon sacrificing his own daughter to another 'god', 'Tantum religio potuit suadere malorum.' – 'So many evils could religion induce.'

And so I struggled with my conscience and my intelligence, and the religion I had inherited by the circumstance of birth – and it seemed to me they were often in opposition.

So I welcomed the cold draught of rational thought that school reintroduced on a Monday morning – and the homely visits to my Granda Roberts that had always meant so much to me.

So Sunday School and the rest of it, for me, wasn't so much an introduction to God, as an introduction to the notion of Evil and the absence of innocence.

Before that time, so far as I can recall, I was genuinely (and innocently) happy.

From that time on the 'flying' at bedtime stopped – and I began wetting the bed instead.

I do remember one positive religious experience from my childhood though:

At about the age of eleven, I was taken, willingly or unwillingly, to the Grosvenor Hall near the city centre, to hear a young visiting preacher who had a reputation as a sort of home-grown Billy Graham (I can't remember his name). And an amazing thing happened. All I can recall from his sermon is his saying at some point, 'The Cross is a stumbling block'* – and somehow for me all that sad, bloody, tortured, Middle-eastern history seemed to fall away and be put in context: as irrelevant to my world *and* a distraction from the real and revolutionary teachings of Jesus – to try to understand and have compassion for others, to 'love' your neighbours instead of killing them.

My Uncle Jack, my cousin David's father, was caretaker of Berry Street Presbyterian Church at the time. We went to visit them afterwards and I remember David and I being allowed to fly our rubber band-powered model aeroplane in the huge, still space of the empty church. But despite this great indulgence from the adults, I felt quite detached, quite un-childlike really, as though I'd stumbled on something of such inexpressible importance that it made even being allowed to play in the church seem commonplace.

And later I walked through the streets with a real and deep, if melancholy, joy. The world, though grey and sad, was also beautiful and profound and infinitely changing. There was no need for those old lead weights of dogma – the true was true without them.

And so I was saved. From the excesses of religion. By the preacher.

---

*My *Chambers Dictionary of Etymology* gives 'stumbling block, 1526, in the Tyndale Bible, something likely to cause moral downfall'. So he was a *very* radical young preacher indeed.

Seven

SO ANYWAY, I SUPPOSE GRANDA GEPP represented the gloomiest side of my young life, and Granda Roberts the lightest. Yet both had suffered similar losses.

Granda Roberts never went to church or Mission Hall – he would walk up and down the living room on a Sunday sometimes, with his hands clasped behind his back, humming a hymn to himself or listening to the radio.

He loved the voice of John McCormack, who sang the *Irish Melodies* of Thomas Moore from the early 1800s; and Delia Murphy singing that beautiful, wistful, witty old song about love and patience, 'The Spinning Wheel'.

During the war he had listened to music from Germany and France and wherever. Music was the same to us all, he said.

Uncle Sammy, his only son (he had four daughters as well), had lived with Granda since returning from London after the war. He had worked in Heavy Rescue, and had narrowly avoided being killed several times as he pulled Londoners out of holes in the ground. So he was a bit put out when somebody said to him – because of his Belfast accent – something like, 'Oi, woy dahn't you speak the fahin King's English, might?'

Uncle Sammy was every child's best friend, and, like his mother before him, a friend of other animals too. He had had a cat, which would meet him halfway back from the linen mill where he worked. When the whistle blew for the dinner break or the end of the working day, the cat would go to meet him and perch on his shoulder for the journey home.

I remember my boyish pleasure at the discovery that some of the bollards, used at the end of the cobbled 'entries' on the other side of Electric Street, were really cannon from the

Napoleonic wars, spiked and pointing skywards. How is it that time puts a romance on bloody warfare? How far back in history it seemed too, that, as Granda told me, the police barracks had been sandbagged and had a machine gun on the roof, in those first Troubles, long before I was born.

Like all the other houses in Electric Street, Granda's had two bedrooms upstairs (you walked through one to get to the other) and a living room and 'working kitchen' downstairs. The working kitchen was an ordinary room with a gas cooker, but with no sink or plumbing.

The sink was a shallow stone one, and it and the solitary brass cold-water tap were in the scullery – a sort of corridor that ran beside the kitchen to the back yard. The high brick wall of the yard had a wooden door opening to the cobbled entry that ran between the backs of the two rows of houses. This door was used to deliver the coal, to put the corrugated metal dustbin out to be emptied by the binmen, and so on. On one side of the yard was the outside toilet. It smelled of whitewash, which came off on hands and clothes if you touched the walls. There was a porcelain toilet bowl mostly hidden by a smooth plank on top. The plank went across the width of the lavatory and had a finely crafted hole cut in it at the business position. A wooden handle and a chain ran to the high flushing tank on the wall behind. Hanging within hand's reach was a sheaf of newspaper, cut to size and strung through a hole in the corner of each sheet. You had to crumple the newspaper to soften it before use. At some point in time the newspaper got replaced by 'Izal' paper on a roll – not a big improvement.

Two doors up from Granda's yard, on the other side of Edi Cochrane's, was Mr Schofield's pigeon loft. I remember being taken up into it once – it felt like a rare and privileged event – and being shown a pigeon's egg. But it was a bit overwhelming too, and the loft felt very high above the ground.

Mr Schofield was from England. He had been wounded in 1915 and his life saved by the Germans who overran his position and took the unconscious man prisoner.

He returned to Belfast, where he had been garrisoned, and married the girl he had met from County Tyrone, who had written to him faithfully during the three and a half years he had spent in the POW camp.

He carried some of the deadly detritus of battle with him for the rest of his life – shrapnel fragments in his leg and back; a bullet lodged in his head, too dangerous to remove.

He was a short man and had the upright bearing of an old soldier, but limped from the shrapnel wounds. As the British army decreed at the time that if you could walk, talk and hold a rifle, you were medically fit, he was not eligible for any allowances. So he drove a tram on the well-to-do Malone Road route. People there were kind to the convalescent soldier and helped him support his family with gifts of bacon and fruit and vegetables, and things for his children. He and his wife would have five children. One of their daughters, Anna, would marry a nephew of my Granda's, and, in the way that families simplify complicated relationships, they had become our Aunt Anna and Uncle Jack.

Like my Granda, Mr Schofield was adored by his grandchildren. Many years later when he died, his youngest grandchild, who was four years old, was told, to comfort him, that God had taken his Granda.

'I HATE GOD!' the child had shouted through his tears.

With a piece of firewood and his Senior Service packet for sails and some matches for masts, Uncle Sammy would sit by the fire and whittle me a galleon. It would take me far away from where I launched it in the gutter of that quiet, cobbled street (though it was inclined to capsize if any *real* wind caught the cardboard sails).

There were no cars in Electric Street.

But Uncle Sammy was tired by War and the loss of his mother. One evening he went up to Auntie Sally's house, near Tates Avenue, to help with wallpapering. He finished the work, sat down on the settee, sighed and died.

I prayed, with a ferocity that would have made angels weep, for Uncle Sammy to come back to life. After all, I was still young enough to have total faith – Jesus had raised up the dead man in the Bible, so why not Uncle Sammy? I suppose I only stopped when he was in the ground, otherwise it could have got a bit awkward for him.

We loved Uncle Sammy dearly, and I remember his best friend, Bobby, was the first grown man I had ever seen who couldn't hold back the tears, and I remember thinking all the better of him for that.

Eight

'FINAGHY," MR COLBERT SAID, '*BallyFinaghy:* the townland of the bog cotton, in the Irish.' Mr Colbert was most children's favourite teacher at Finaghy Primary School, though Mrs Johnson, my very first teacher, was another favourite – a sweet natured motherly woman. Mr Colbert's translation was a poetic one, as the reference books say 'Baile an Fhionnachaidh' is the 'townland of the white field' – but why else would the field be white, if not for the bog cotton, growing not far from the River Lagan – Abhainn an Lagáin – 'the river of the low-lying area'?

My mother and father had moved to Finaghy when I was about two years old.

They rented a terraced house, in a row of four, with a small garden in front and a larger one behind, on a big 'Housing Trust' estate. It had been built in the late forties and there may have been one other family there before us, as I have a vague memory of some childish scribbles left on a bare plaster wall by a window.

Our mothers would walk with the youngest children to school in the morning and come to pick us up again at the end of the school day.

Up Benmore to the school we went, with the 'Big Field' and its groups of old oaks on our left, following the school railings until we turned left again (where another oak tree grew on a stone-walled island) into Torr Way and the school gates.

If we were lucky we might meet Mr Reavy on the way, an old man with a dark brown overcoat and hat, and a face healthy red like an apple, who would pretend to chase us with his walking stick. 'Chase *me*, Mr Reavy, chase *me*!'

School was a mixed blessing. In early days it was a time of great pleasure. I remember the joy of painting a backdrop for some sort of table-top desert around Christmastime. It probably had varnished Plasticine, or papier-mâché, models of the Three Kings on camels in the sand in front. I mixed the powder paints and layered them on the big sheet of paper – yellows at the bottom, going up through oranges to reds and a rich deep blue. A desert sunset for the wise ones – and the first time I was aware of the power of pigment and colour. And of being separate somehow, from the final creation, which became more than I could have known or intended. I loved it, not because *I* had done it (though I was pleased I had) but because it was beautiful, and that beauty came from the thing itself – I had just put the pigments together; *it* was more than the sum of the parts. I didn't analyse it in that way, but I *felt* the surprise of it, that more than-ness of it, the joy of it.

And it is still how I feel about creative work.

However, school seemed to get more serious after a while; and, always the gullible one, I believed everything I was told and worked hard to be first in the class and things like that. (To be second was disappointing, and to be fourth, which happened one year, seemed a serious failure.)

But I was also aware of children being 'bad', getting away with mischief and having a lot more fun.

(The sort of 'bad boy' jokes that made us snigger at Finaghy

Primary School were mostly scatological and went something like this: Schoolboy to French teacher, 'Please Miss, can I go to the toilet?' Teacher, 'Oui, oui.' Schoolboy, 'No, plop, plop!'

Or, in an attempt to embarrass another child – who had to be bright enough to know what was inferred, not often the case – someone would shout, 'Here wee fella, you dropped somethin' ... too late, the flies are on it!')

So, one day in a spirit of reckless rebellion, I threw a sweetie cigarette packet out of the school window from my desk when the teacher wasn't looking. When I got home, though, my timidity returned and I got to worrying about my serious crime against the litter rules. I tried hard to get a cold to avoid going to school the next day (the simple technique of putting a feather from the pillow up your nose was effective).

Anyway, I did have the next day off, and gradually realised how silly I had been to worry about such a tiny thing.

Returning to school the following morning, everything was fine, until, at the end of the day, Mrs Stewart (not as nice as Mrs Johnson) says, 'David Gepp, there was a sweet packet thrown out of the window near your desk, so you will please see that it doesn't happen again.' I went bright red in front of the whole class. That was me; I never got away with anything.

So I quickly returned to being the studious type again.

Credulity and innocence can sometimes be positive qualities though. I hated the competitive sports – my spirit was never in it – but one year I managed to win the race on Sports Day. And that was down to divine intervention, or superstition, or my blind belief in my father. He saw how worried I was about the inevitability of being last, so he told me he had some Magic Running Powder that made you go faster. He put it in my running shoes – my 'gutties'. Straight out of the talcum tin. I ran like a rocket, without a care in the world.

There's a boy I see, on the way home from school about this time. Hard done by, pinched face, bogies. He's waiting for me at the end of his front garden path. 'D'you wanna fight?' he says. 'No thanks,' says I – the thought of knuckle on bone had always made me feel queasy. 'Come on,' he says, 'I'll fight you!' 'Well,' I say, resigning myself, 'I'll fight you if you can spell encyclopaedia' (which was the biggest word I knew).

'E-N-S-' he says. 'No, that's wrong,' I say, and go on my way, unharmed.

And every day he's there waiting for me, and every day he spells it wrong. And if he'd ever got it right I'd have had a quare hiding. He would believe me when I said he was wrong, and I would tell him when he was right, of course; those were the Rules.

There was another boy whose name I remember, but won't mention in case he's a bishop or something. He had a wee gang round in Benmore that we avoided. Anyway, there he is one day in front of our house, pulling lumps out of the privet hedge. I go down the garden path and say, 'You'd better stop that!'

'Why,' says he, 'what will you do?'

'Nothing,' I says, 'you'd just better stop it."

'I'll hit you!' he says.

Here's me (like an eejit): 'See if I care.'

So he hits me hard, right in the face with his fist.

Through the stars I hear myself, quite cool:

'Huh, *that* didn't hurt' – with just enough scorn in my voice to worry him.

He turns on his heels and runs – I think he thought he'd met Superman.

And then I went into the house, put my head in a cushion and moaned and groaned and cried to myself with the pain.

My friend Norman's father drove a lorry, which was parked sometimes outside their house. (It would be one of only two or three vehicles in the long street.) We would clamber into the back to play, using the wheels and metal mudguards as footholds. It was a tipper lorry with a dented open-topped back about three feet deep and a locking flap at the rear to dump the load when it tipped.

From inside this shallow fortress we could ambush friends with imaginary gunfire – or just sit until we got bored. It smelled of crusted earth, or had a gritty dusting of sand, depending on the last load.

Friday was payday for most people then, and Norman's father always brought him a bag of sweets home – Crunchie Bars, Caramacs, Toffee Cups (my favourite), Love Hearts, Spangles, Wagon Wheels. Although Norman was always generous I still remember feeling the smallest twinge of envy. Like he was rich (if only in sweets) and I wondered why I wasn't.

Norman and I are playing in his porch, three doors down the street from our house. It's a damp, dismal day, and we're making the best of it. We're playing with small plastic figures – a grey deep-sea diver and a green archer I remember, from a mixed collection he kept in a shoebox.

You put the deep-sea diver into a lemonade bottle filled with water, and there's a bubble forms in his face mask. As you screw down the hard rubber stopper the bubble gets smaller and he drops to the bottom, and, as you loosen it, up he comes again.

Norman's mother comes out, looks at the drizzle and says, 'It's rainin' the day because they're hangin' a woman in England.'

It just seemed another part of that dull grey day.

It must have been the 13th July 1955.

We were seven, Ruth Ellis, (the woman they hanged) was twenty-eight.

I went to Ballyhalbert with Norman and his mother and his Auntie Ginny one year. We stayed in a cottage just across the narrow road from the sea wall. It was the first time I had smelled camping gas. I remember the toilet bucket being emptied over the sea wall, Mrs Sames trying to avoid the gusts of wind that blew it back!

But sometimes memory is an ambivalent thing. It can be triggered unwantedly and unwittingly in so many ways, yet at other times elude our grasp if we do not approach it firmly or tenderly, depending on its nature. Sometimes a smell (and how profound and powerful that can be), sometimes a taste or a transient sound or sight, can remind us, re-place a part of us into an earlier state. And sometimes (if very occasionally) it can be a tactile thing – the feeling of fingers on a chalkboard. Or it may be an emotion or a feeling, that dips us into the past, like a stone skimming the deep pool of our memories; so that the ripples reaching the shore of our consciousness may seem different, unexpected, depending on the stone we throw and where we stand on the shore when they reach us.

Is the well we have to draw from changeable, when the life that has filled it to now is unchangeable? I think not. But the secrets of the process of memory are still hidden from me.

I remember, for example, the first touch of melancholy in my young life.

A boy who lived in the next street died of an illness, I don't know what. We were about the same age, seven or eight, I suppose.

The neighbourhood was not so much shocked or saddened at his death – it seems to me now – as *disappointed* that such a thing could still happen, after a war had been fought and so many social systems forced to change. (Child mortality and illiteracy had become rarities, rather than the commonplace of my father's and grandfathers' generations. The National Health Service had been introduced in the year of my birth and education to any level was now free on merit.)

I remember this boy's funeral – or I *think* I remember it – and this may be the strangest paradox of memory – not *un*true and yet impossible. For I remember the same event twice.

Once I am sitting at my desk in Finaghy Primary School, looking out of the window towards Torr Way, as they carry his coffin past the school railings.

And then again, I am at home sick, and from the kitchen window I see it pass by on the silent street.

Is one version of events a mirage of the mind – the daydream of a child – remembered in parallel, and with the same intensity, as the other reality?

I have only one certainty – only one child died. So my memory is an unreliable witness. But it may still touch me with other strange, deep, and unsettling truths.

Nine

ONCE A YEAR THEY CUT THE grass in the Big Field. The children would all go up there and build a sort of igloo that we called a 'grass house' and which we would defend against all comers.

We would have 'grass fights' – throwing fistfuls of grass at one another, running round, squealing – euphoric from the smell of cut grass and burying ourselves in it.

On the way home from school one day we had a grass fight, and grass spilled over onto the road. One of the men cutting shouted at us, and told me to clean it up.

When I'd left my school bag off at home, and come back, he wasn't there. But I was still picking up the wisps of grass, at dusk, when he walked past on his way home.

'Is that alright, Mister?' I asked, tired out. 'I suppose so,' he said, probably surprised to see me there at all. What a poor, stupid, good child I was.

As the Talmud says: 'Heaven doesn't approve when we sin, and the world doesn't approve when we are virtuous.'

After the grass was cut the white clover would appear, and we would pull the flowers apart and suck the drops of sweet nectar, lying in the sunshine, in that perfectly relaxed way of childhood – when there was a world of grown-ups to do all the other stuff.

Around this time I was left in the house on my own for the first time, while my mother went to the shops (a ten minute walk away). I had been there, drawing, or something like that, for a while. It was in the deep silence that could envelop the world in those rare car, no television, wirelesses that took ages to warm up, sort of days.

I started to notice that I could hear breathing. At first I thought it was my own, but when I stopped and listened it just carried on. In - out, in - out, 'uh - huh, uh - huh, uh - huh'. Keeping very quiet I tried to work out where it was coming from. There was no place for anyone to hide in the living room where I was playing, so I went to the foot of the stairs and listened there. It wasn't coming from upstairs, which left the kitchen and the back hall, and the cupboard under the stairs. Holding my own breath so as not to be heard I went in that direction, and it became clearer and louder, 'UH-HUH, UH-HUH, UH-HUH'. It wasn't coming from the kitchen on my left, but from the cupboard under the stairs. My chest thumped as I held my breath and turned the key in the cupboard door and drew it open towards me. There was the electric meter, the disc rubbing slowly as it turned, 'uh-huh, uh-huh, uh-huh'.

Sometimes in the summer we would go 'up to the country' – mostly Banbridge and Gilford way – to visit relatives of my Granda Roberts, including our Great Aunts Mary-Ann and Sarah-Jane. They lived in a terrace of low, slated cottages, which were immaculately clean, with polished iron ranges and tiled or flagged floors.

I can remember one of them taking us all round to see another relative, a tall, upright, singular sort of woman – a bit younger than the Great Aunts. I forget her name. I think she must have thought her house looked too artificially cleaned up for visitors, so she spat cheerfully on the tiled floor with some ceremony, as though to loosen things up, and say, 'Relax, it's not always this tidy.' The aunties said, 'Oh don't do that now, dear' in the maternal tones you'd use with somebody who was a bit lacking. But to me she seemed independent, and a rebel against the niceties. I was grateful to her for changing things, for the unexpected, for cheering me up.

Our visits to the country were the only times we would get to meet our Catholic relatives ('the Opposite Faith', as it was called!) None of them lived in the city.

I suppose our favourite visit of all was to Mary Walsh. She had a sweetie shop in Banbridge, and gave us ice-creams and chocolate, while the grown-ups had tea in the back, and Mary jumped up to serve customers if the shop bell rang.

Great Aunt Sarah-Jane was very old, and I was taken up to visit her on her deathbed. The skin on her hands was fine and transparent, her white hair rolled up.

I didn't know she was on her deathbed, and I don't know what she said; but I've always felt I was given something, that

I was blessed by her, at that meeting. A gift of the very old to the very young. Maybe it was the gift of how to die well – the same gift we need to live well.

My mother went to Great Aunt Sarah-Jane's funeral. A muted bell was tolled in that country way, as they shuffled quietly, heads covered and bent, behind the coffin.

The bell got on my mother's nerves.

When I was about nine or ten I had to go to the dentist near Finaghy Crossroads to have a tooth out.

It would be my first experience of a drug-induced state, and not one I would find myself wanting to repeat.

I remember I had to bite on a cube of black rubber, with a chain attached (to stop you swallowing it, presumably). Then a mask, with a corrugated rubber tube running to the tanks of gas, was put over my nose and mouth.

I remember being told to breathe deeply, and then feeling I was somehow on the *outside* of the tube, and then, suddenly I was *inside* it. I went down and down and down. I was in a cavern underneath a volcano. There was a lake (of water) there, strangely – and, I think, a boat of some sort. But the scariest thing was the archetypal, ancient woman, who lived on an island of sorts, the red of the volcano somehow active around it. The image of the Archetype has been excised from my mind, both as child and adult; I have no memory of her appearance. But the experience was terrifying and awesome and belittling.

Then, there I was, terrified, but somewhere else too, and someone was saying, 'Where are you, David? Are you on a seat on the number 59 bus?' I struggled to answer such a *stupid* question, because it was the one place I knew I wasn't, and there I was, groggily and insistently back in the dentist's chair.

There seemed to be a smiling sense of relief in the room. I remember the nurse hovering with some water – she may have been splashing it on my face.

I remember leaving with my friend Norman (who had come with me and must have waited for me) and saying to him loudly, as we walked off home past the dentist's open window, 'THE NUMBER 59 BUS HONEST TO GOODNESS!' as though I hadn't been fooled or confused for a second.

The terror I had felt at the dentist's had only been matched once before in my young life.

That earlier terror, when I was still an infant, had been caused by a recurring dream. Visually it was a strangely Victorian sort of thing, like a Kate Greenaway watercolour – but timeless.

In deep silence, and always in colour, I would see an

androgynous child – dressed in some kind of smock and holding a bunch of balloons – skipping across rounded green hills. Then, at some point, the child released the balloons. The dream always repeated itself exactly, and always ended at the same point. And I would always wake up screaming.

I didn't know it was a classically Freudian castration dream at the time, of course.

And maybe that is what amplifies terror – the lack of any understanding of what we are experiencing.

It is not easy being a child – and that is something we *all* too readily forget, as we grow older.

Ten

THE DAY BEFORE RUTH ELLIS WAS killed would have been the 12th July. This was a big day in Finaghy as it was where all the Orangemen marched to – to 'The Field' (which was up Finaghy Road North somewhere, beyond Finaghy station). The night before was called 'The Eleventh Night', and was a strange, primitive mix, with the echo of the huge Lambeg drums rolling down the darkening Lagan valley, and the burning of giant bonfires – often with an effigy of the Pope (or Lundy, the Governor of Derry) on the top. If our parents allowed us to, we would throw potatoes into the embers. When they were burnt to charcoal on the outside, we poked them out with sticks and carefully peeled them, put salt on them and ate them steaming hot, burning our fingers all the while. No matter how well you tried to peel them there were always still flecks of crunchy, black carbon left sticking to the potatoes, giving them a great burnt, woodsmoke taste.

We never went to the Field on 'the Twelfth', but the whole family would go to watch the procession at the Crossroads, with the thousands of other people lining the road from Belfast three or four deep, some carrying chairs or stools, the children often sitting on the kerb at the front.

First would come the strange old men with sandwich boards, or aprons, printed in white on black, PREPARE TO MEET THY DOOM and stuff like that. Some would preach and harangue the crowd as they walked, and wave their Bibles to make some point.

There was a sense of relief when they had passed and the fun could start.

Pipe bands and flute bands (led by young men who could catch a big baton thrown twenty foot in the air while somersaulting in between) and 'kilties' from Scotland were greeted with cheers. People called out to the individual Orangemen, as they marched by with military precision: 'There's our Jimmy.' And a nod and a smile, as they marched on, or marked time if there was a delay somewhere in front.

There were big silk banners with orange and silver borders, painted with scenes of past battles, from the Boyne to the Somme. Or images of Protestant martyrs – like Archbishop Latimer and Nicholas Ridley, being burned to death, with Latimer's words: 'We shall this day light such a candle, by God's Grace, in England as I trust shall never be put out.'

Or a portrait of some Orange notable from the past, 'Brother William McKinley' or something like that.

Some men marched with ceremonial swords, some at the edge with some sort of spears or pikes. Some carried small wooden gavels and books. I think they all wore bowler hats.

Others held the ornamental ropes from the tops and bottoms of the banners, so the whole crew, if it was a windy day, had to sail like a land boat with twelve feet. The banners would billow, the silver and pigments catch the sun, and it was spectacular indeed.

To the grown-ups who had lived through a war and the dull, monotone scarcities of life afterwards, with its ration books and lack of colour (for war is a strange brightly coloured, if empty, time), it must have seemed a welcome contrast. To us it was a carnival. It was there that I sat in the sun on the kerb's edge, wiping the juice from my chin, as I tasted the first peach I had ever eaten, bought from one of the sellers who moved through the crowds.

Who would have thought those butterfly wings of fluttering banners could intensify into a venomous vortex of hate-filled rhetoric – the dark thundercloud that would provoke a truculent and hate-filled echo of itself, and blow this part of Ireland into a whirlwind cycle of accusation and justification and violence – like the destructive fugue of a murderous marriage?

Did some, even then, in those sun-filled days, have the ugliness in their hearts? For if the ugliness was not in hearts then, it lived on like a deadly virus in the culture.

There it could assume a cheerful – even colourful – mask for years to come, until its demonic qualities were summoned up by a different kind of preacher.

For I can see young factory girls, arms linked and wearing funny hats, walking down Sandy Row, cheerfully and artlessly singing:

> We are, we are, we are the Billy Boys,
> We are, we are, we are the Billy Boys,
> We're up to our necks in Fenian blood,
> Surrender or you'll die,
> For we, we are the Billy Boys.

And so it would take most of the morning for the procession to pass. And most of the afternoon for it to return to Belfast. There were at least a couple of hours in between, when we would all hurry home and have a long lunch. Most of the Orangemen stayed on the Field, where they had speeches and sandwiches – with beer, or tea or lemonade – depending on whether they were in a 'Temperance' Lodge or not.

Our family had no Orange connections on either my mother or father's side, but my Aunt Sally's husband, Uncle Jim, was an Orangeman, so he would come round with his best friend Ernest to our house for lunch, along with the other aunties and uncles who would come up for the day. Lunch was a special occasion on the Twelfth.

'Portballintrae' would be brought out to cope with the demand for tea. Portballintrae was a huge, brown enamelled teapot, which came from the village of the same name on the north Antrim coast, where my parents had stayed on their honeymoon.

They were both twenty-three when they married.

They had been so inundated with visitors that they bought it from a local shop to make tea for everyone. My cousin Maureen, who was ten, and was my mother's bridesmaid, liked the place so much that she stayed with them for the rest of their honeymoon!

The talk at lunch on the Twelfth would be of holidays.

Uncle Jim, Auntie Sally and Elizabeth nearly always went to Bangor. We would go to the Isle of Man – often with Auntie Annie and Uncle John, or Auntie Ivy. And the prospects for the weather, and children would be teased and pocket money handed out. (This came weekly, regular as clockwork, in threepenny and sixpenny bits, from the Uncles and Grandas. If we missed seeing them one week, there would be two weeks' money the next time.)

'Anybody want more apple tart – or tea?'

'Can I have a wee bit more of that barmbrack there?'

Then Portballintrae would be taken into the kitchen and rinsed out and put away until the next big gathering. (The tea leaves would go with the rest of the refuse into the smelly bucket under the big white sink – which was *never* called a

Belfast sink in Belfast – and every week the 'Refuse Man' would come up the street with his pony and cart, empty the bucket in with the rest of the swill and take it off somewhere to feed his pigs and chickens.)

At school I showed no skill in music (in the infants' band I was given the triangle to hit on a nod from the teacher) – except for singing, which I loved. I sang everywhere.

Until one day I was seated upstairs at my business, with my back to the window, which had the top flap open, when I heard a shout from some children outside, 'Here wee fella, what're you doing singing on the toilet?!' I can remember to this day how red I went, and still feel the echo of the shame. Another bit of innocence lost.

The docks in Belfast were busy, noisy, overwhelming in scale in those days. Strangely, they seemed a long way from the sea – with concrete-patched, wide cobbled areas and iron tram and

crane tracks to step over. Our father would carry our two cases
to the quay where the ferry to the Isle of Man waited. The only
glimpse you got of the sea before sailing was the flotsam-
scattered tarry gap, between rusted waterline and shore, that
made you shudder at the thought of falling, as you climbed the
swaying ramp into the belly of the boat.

The steamships were tiny compared to today's car ferries.
They had names like *Mona's Isle* and *Lady of Mann* and *Ben-
my-Chree*. I remember slatted benches, wooden life rafts and
lifeboats, and soot-blackened red funnels – and men sitting
drinking, with crates of porter.

As we sailed out into the Irish Sea some would get sick and
drunk, and empty bottles would roll about the metal gutters.
Those old ships burnt coal, and their black smoke was blown
off to the lee, the smoke from other ships visible on the horizon.

The seamen seldom appeared, and it seemed a peculiarly
self-contained and independent world, parallel to, but seldom
touching, the world of those who lived on land.

But, romantic as it sometimes seemed, the sea broad and the
sky infinite, more often than not, to children on a crowded and
uncomfortable boat, it was a journey to be endured as much as
enjoyed.

We always stayed in Douglas, which is where the ferry docked in the Isle of Man. The strong smell of the brewery would often cover parts of the town, mingling with the air from the sea.

That yeasty, sweet-sickly smell is present as I watch the first flying ants I had seen land on the coping stones outside Mrs Kelly's boarding house, wander about a bit – and, there was no doubt about it – PULL THEIR OWN WINGS OFF!

In Douglas I spent most of my saved pocket money on a toy yacht 'designed by Uffa Fox' which Uncle John and I sailed for happy hours on the boating pond on the promenade. We sailed it across to one another, turning it round and into the wind when it approached the edge and within reach of our long, white wood boathooks, sometimes catching the hook in the rigging instead and causing a capsize.

Another year I bought a light green, clockwork, metal submarine (modelled on Jules Verne's *Nautilus*). It had a rubber bung with a copperwire 'periscope' on it, which you removed to wind it up. It dived until the winding ran out, and then bobbed unpredictably to the surface somewhere. We would then have the fun and frustration of bringing it to shore by a lot of splashing and shouting and stretching with our boathooks.

At dusk we might all take the horse tram down to the 'Fairy Glen', where we children were happy to be amused by lights going on and off inside individual plastic squirrels, sequenced so that they seemed to run up into the trees.

We were also taken to the shop, one street back from the promenade, where they made the seaside rock, and watched with cool disinterest as they spun the words DOUGLAS IOM into a hooked and spinning mountain of pink and white candy. Now I have no idea how it was done. I wish I had paid attention.

At the end of the holiday we would bring back bars of this rock, and painted plaster models of the Tower of Refuge (a sort of castle in the sea in Douglas Bay) as gifts.

One of these models of the Tower of Refuge sat – almost forever – on the mantelpiece at home.

I don't think my mother was very fond of housework, but she was quite house-proud, and liked things clean and tidy. It was probably because of this that we didn't have plants – 'dust traps' – in the house, and we weren't allowed pets. Except for white mice. They came from the pet shop near the Crossroads, and they had to be kept in the 'back hall' (the unplastered corridor, with the coal store, that led from the front to the back garden).

Carole and I were told they were our responsibility, but I can remember the occasional tang of mouse pee from their cage, so I expect we didn't clean them as often as we should. But they seemed to thrive.

I think our mother was initially persuaded that we should be allowed to keep mice by my father, who had always had pets when he was a boy – a dog called Jack, cats, and white mice. He believed the latter were underrated as interesting and intelligent creatures.

He had kept his mice, in a cage with a sliding plywood door, on a table at home in Euterpe Street. One night he was sitting up late doing a correspondence course and saw one of his mice push up the sliding door and escape, running down the table leg, along the hall and squeezing under the front door. One of the neighbours had been complaining about having mice, '... but they were white', but my father didn't see the connection until the mouse reappeared later, nudged the sliding door up and went inside the cage again, leaving no evidence (except for the evidence of my delighted father's eyes) of its night time travels.

Our mice were never quite as bright or interesting as that (or maybe they just couldn't manage the more secure door on the house my father had built them) but, like all animals, they were amazing in unique ways. They bred, well, like mice. One little pink blob was born with a back foot almost half the size of his whole body (probably because we had allowed them to inbreed out of ignorance). Anyway, he had this until he was weaned and grew fur, and then, one morning, we came down to find the foot in a corner of the cage, and 'Hopalong' as he would always be known, skipping about quite happily with his brothers and sisters. Whether he did the surgery himself, or his mother had done it, we never knew.

At Hatch's, the hardware shop at the Crossroads, we boys would buy bamboo canes for a few pennies and tie them with string to make bows (though they'd always have more of a curl at the thin end). As arrows we could fire the stripped-off stems of Golden Rod, but they would split from the pressure of the string, and after a few goes were hopeless.

When I was a bit older I took some saved-up pocket money to the Athletic Stores in the city centre, and bought a couple of real archery arrows, with blunt brass heads, feathers and a notch for the string. They flew a long way with a bamboo bow.

Norman and I played a game where one of us would go across the Big Field at the top of the street and the other would fire an arrow to see how far we could get it. We invented a game where we would roll out of the way of the arrow. Anyway, I fired an arrow. I knew it was a good long shot, but Norman, lying in the grass, thought it would be the same as the last one. So, to my horror, I see him, and can see him still, rolling away from me. And the arrow in the air – and him and it about to meet. I have my hands to my head; if I shout a warning he'll only look up and get it in the eye. And that's it – he's face down on the grass with an arrow in his back – I've killed my best friend and Time Has Stopped.

Then the arrow falls over. He's looking over his shoulder where there's a pink dent in the skin. He laughs. Neither of us ever tells anybody.

Despite my unwitting attempts to put him off the track, Norman had persevered with his enquiries into the making of babies. He had older brothers and began to acquire snippets of information. Like it is called seX because the boy lies on top of the girl like an X – and to make a baby, you spit in her mouth – eeugh! We laugh in disgusted delight at it all.

But many questions were still unanswered. One day, while we were up in the Big Field by the school railings, Erica Mahoney, an older girl (by at least two years), decided to enlighten us all. (I remember that she was perched on top of the railings).

Babies, she declared, were made when 'the man's horse goes into the woman's stable'.

'Ah!' we nodded wisely. As though we understood perfectly. And that was it for another while.

Norman and I had been less innocent – and even more naive – some time before. We had climbed onto the window sill (the toilet window was glazed with a sort of clear bubble glass, that you couldn't see anything through that was any distance away)

and, lifting the top flap a bit, had peered out at the street below, somehow thinking we were invisible, though we were pushed up against the window and were as visible as if the glass were clear.

Mrs O'Grady, our neighbour, came along, and Norman, the wickedness on him, whispers, 'I dare you to shout "O'Grady balls,"' so I shout it through the flap and we both hunker down and snigger at our daring, secure in our invisibility. Well, there's a knock on the door and a short conversation between Mrs O'Grady and my mother.

Norman is sent home and I'm sent round to Mrs O'Grady to say sorry, the backs of my legs still stinging from the slap I'd got from my mother – which I deserved as much for the stupidity of thinking we were invisible, as the rudeness.

Up to then I had no idea that the word 'balls' had any insulting or biological meaning that fell outside the world of the football, and even after a smacking I don't think I was any the wiser.

So weeks and months and seasons passed. The year was measured by the Easter and summer holidays and Christmastime.

The best was the summer holiday – eight or ten weeks of

play and freedom. Picnics and grass fights. Going on expeditions to the Wee Woods or the Big Woods, our brightly-coloured toy canteens full of sun-warmed, plastic-tainted water. Visits to the Big Woods had an added air of excitement, as childish legend had it that someone had once found, in the field by the convent wall, a spiked German helmet from the First World War. Our (historically uninformed) imaginations were inspired by the thought of a similar discovery – or even hand grenades or something.

War games seem to have been a big part of our play in those days.

I had acquired a good set of accessories, mostly from my Granda's attic in Euterpe Street: a WWI bandolier for bullets, a (full-sized) tin hat, a gas mask, two ancient bayonets in leather and brass scabbards, and a broken air rifle that had belonged to my cousin Jim. Robert Parker had a BB gun that didn't fire anything, but made a great bang and a ricochet sound: and a realistic (to us) machine gun on a tripod. So we pulled the pins from imaginary grenades and blew one another to imaginary kingdom come with full sound effects ('You're dead!' – 'I'm not, you missed' – 'That grenade didn't go off', etc.).

We arranged ambushes with those who were to be ambushed, and squabbled over who would be Japs or Jerries. I think I was quite bossy, though, and if you were on my side (whichever side that was) you stood a good chance of winning: I had, after all, read (a little of) Field Marshal Montgomery's memoirs.

I wonder now what Mr Mawhinney – not so very long back from being parachuted into France – made of it, as he washed the gardening mud off his hands at the kitchen sink overlooking our battleground.

And there were more leisurely times – lying unseen in the shade in Robert Parker's tent in his back garden, and killing ourselves laughing when his mother said over the fence to a neighbour, 'I'm all behind today.'

Don't those remembered summers seem forever sunny and blue-skied?

In the daytime we had bicycle rides to the 'Minnieburn' near Shaw's Bridge – going timidly through Taughmonagh and the prefabs that we called 'The Bungalows', where the kids had a reputation for toughness, and pedalling across the main road to Dub Lane and through Barnett's Park.

You would sometimes see the boys from the bungalows down by the Lagan Weir, shouting and jumping naked into the water; and you hoped you wouldn't catch their attention, as you veered away from their wilder freedom.

In the evenings, you went to bed when it was still light, and would sometimes hear the oddly comforting drone of a single aeroplane on its way to land at Nutt's Corner.

Like most city-born children, we were wasteful of nature when we found it. We would come back from the woods with armfuls of bluebells that soon died, or minnows from the Minnowburn that would not survive long, and newts, or caterpillars or tadpoles – victims of the careless curiosity of small humans.

We ran about stripped to the waist in the sun, and, if it looked like your skin was red your mother would rub on olive oil, out of a small bottle from Beggs the Chemist or the Co-op in Sicily Park – or butter if she had no oil. So you were cooked nicely.

If you came across a dead animal while you were exploring, there was a ritual that had to be followed. You would gather round, in that solemn way of children, maybe somebody would poke it with a stick; then, as you left, you had to spit lightly, to avoid 'The Disease'.

In the middle of the square at the rear of our houses, surrounded by the back gardens, was a field that was later drained for garages to be built.

We called this 'the Wee Field' and it was a damp corrupted bit of old bogland, where the bog cotton no longer grew, only rushes and sharp grasses in the squelchy ground. There were daddy-long-legs and 'clegs' there – flies that sucked your blood – and other rust red insects. And ugly black and red-segmented larvae of some sort.

So we didn't play in the Wee Field often. But sometimes we were lucky and saw young frogs there, an inch or two long, which we caught in our hands and looked at, fascinated, and then let jump free again.

A few doors down from our house was Mrs Thompson's lamp post. Shaped like a skinny, concrete question mark, it usually had a rope attached somewhere near the top where the girls would swing around it like a maypole, sitting in the looped end of the rope – spinning one way until the rope was twined high around the post, and then back out again.

Or they played hopscotch, or skipping:

> On the mountain stands a lady
> Who she is I do not know
> All she wants is gold and silver
> All she wants is a fine young man ...

– while the boys ran about rat-tat-tatting our war games; or ululated, or clicked our mouths for hoof sounds and slapped our bottoms as we galloped around, and jumped over the low garden walls, to take cover as Cowboys or Indians, the air full of the smell and flash and noise of the caps in our guns (if we had had the pennies to buy some).

On the very rare occasions that a posh car would come past on Benmore Drive, the joke was to run along beside it shouting, 'Daddy! Daddy!'

A game that we all played, boys and girls, was Hangoseek – that was what it was called – its origins in 'hide and go seek' long lost.

We selected who was to be 'on it' by lining up, with our two fists out in front, and someone would walk down the line going: 'One potato, two potato, three potato, four; five potato, six potato, seven potato *more*', tapping a fist, as they walked along the line, for each 'potato', and at '*more*', that fist was put behind your back. The child who was 'on it' was the last one left with a fist still out in front. Or we would use 'eeny, meeny, miney, mo' which *was* quicker. (We didn't think of it – '... catch a nigger by the toe' – as racist, a word that didn't exist for us. We lived in ignorant innocence – or innocent ignorance – in too many ways.)

So the child who was 'on it' had to cover their eyes against Mrs Thompson's lamp post and count, very quickly, to the number that had been decided on (generally one hundred) while the others ran to hide: 'Five-ten-fifteen-twenty-twentyfive-thirty-thirtyfive-forty-fortyfive-fifty-fiftyfive-sixty-sixtyfive-seventy-seventyfive-eighty-eightyfive-ninety-ninetyfive-AHUNDRED – here I come away or not and if you're caught it's not my fault.'

This was all watched over with the odd tail wag by Peter, Mrs Thompson's black collie. He was too old to be bothered to join in, but good-natured enough to be fussed.

The only other dog in the neighbourhood was the curly-haired, ratty-tailed, shoe-polish brown Irish Water Spaniel, who lived in Locksley Gardens, but we only ever saw him out walking with his owner. I suppose he was too special to be allowed to wander the streets – he was of a rare, odd but kind-looking, breed.

In Benmore Drive, between our house and the house of the spaniel, lived a boy who had a pet crow. It stayed close to him, but would occasionally fly up to the roofs in a display of independence, and need to be tempted down again with a crust or something.

I got to know this boy a little, and remember how quietly awed I was to be allowed to see this spirited, wild, feathered creature from close to.

Another skipping song from that time is:

> Mammy Daddy Uncle Dick
> Went to London on a stick
> The stick broke
> What a joke
> Mammy Daddy Uncle Dick

And I remember searching for a suitably explosive word; outraged by Marjorie McAffern's refusal to let us boys have the rope again to play lassoes with, 'You ... You BUM!' I splutter.

'Well, David Gepp, I'm going to tell your Mammy on you – you used a dirty word!' she says, mocking with her hand on her hip.

I race her to the door-knocker and hang on to it as she tries to knock. I'm desperate to stop my mother finding out how bad I've been.

My mother hears the commotion and comes to the door. 'Mrs Gepp, your David just called me a BUM!'

Heart in shoes I wait for the thunderstorm. 'Well,' my mother says to her. '*You* shouldn't be telling tales, should you?'

I feel my panic slide away and I'm breathing again – the air of an improved world, which has some unexpected sense and justice in it.

Mrs Thompson's lamp post came into its own in the winter as well. It was the only lamp post for the top end of a long street, the next being Mrs Anderson's halfway down, further than we went to play.

In the dark nights of winter the metallic violet-blue of the lamp would light the first flakes of snow, which whirled in the silence that snow can still bring to our, far noisier, world. Every year Carole and I would drag out the sledge our father had made. It was heavy, with a thick canvas-covered platform, and solid wooden runners, with packing case metal nailed on them, which we waxed with candles. Every year we tried it out, and every year it didn't work – cutting through the snow to the stones of the pavement and refusing to move. So we would sit on it and throw snowballs – for too long sometimes, for, when I went into the house and took my wet gloves off by the coal fire, the pain in my frozen fingers often made me bawl.

A favourite winter treat, though, was our mother's home-made ginger cordial – made with treacly, dark brown sugar from Barbados. It sat, covered with a dish cloth, in the big cream baking bowl before being bottled, and was then diluted with cold tapwater in the tumbler. I remember the swirling gold of the thicker liquid refracting as it dissolved, and the sweet, gingery heat of it as you gulped it down.

In the summer the nearest equivalent we had was shop-bought 'Creamola Foam', from a tin in the larder. We loved this too. You spooned some of the powder into a tumbler of water and it made a bright orange coloured foaming drink, with a white 'head' on top. This was before we had a fridge or ice cubes. We didn't miss what we'd never known, and enjoyed what we did have with the full-hearted enthusiasm of childhood.

I think our father must have given up the idea of building anything more complicated after the very limited success of his sledge, as (unlike many fathers and older brothers in the street) he never made us a 'Guider'.

A Guider was built as a low, wooden platform on old pram wheels. It was important that the front (smaller) wheels could be steered, either by placing your feet on a board that held the axle on a central pivot, or by tying a rope to either end of the board and pulling it to right or left as you sat or lay on the platform. Guiders were very fast. They were powered by pushing with your foot on the ground – or by other children running and pushing you – until you were part-way down the nearest hill and they could no longer keep up. Then they would return to the top and wait for their turn. Some Guiders were small and noisy, with metal ball-bearing wheels in front, and some were silent, big and sleek. They could reach exciting, if not frightening, speeds, and almost always crashed. I never saw one with brakes. If nerves threatened to fail at speed, a child at the back, or a solitary rider lying prone, would try to slow down by putting the soles of their shoes on the road, but that nearly always led to a loss of steering at the front, a shrieking laughter-filled tumble, and a breathless, 'That was BRILLIANT!' (even while rubbing bruised elbows and knees as you hobbled back up the hill).

Hallowe'en was a good time of the year. Children would always dress up then. Our father would blacken a cork on the gas ring, and draw moustaches or beards on our faces if we wanted to be pirates or Dick Turpin, or whatever. Or we might have 'papermashy' false faces from the shops.

We would collect pennies from the doors for fireworks, singing:

> Hallowe'en is coming on
> And the geese are getting fat
> Would you please put a penny in the old man's hat
> If you haven't got a penny a ha'penny will do
> And if you haven't got a ha'penny God bless you
> And your old man too.

Most years we would have a party in our house. The main things were ducking for apples, and lucky dips (in sawdust my father got from Gerry the butcher) and a fruit loaf or barmbrack with silver threepenny bits in it.

Then the moment would come when you would traipse out to the front garden, with the milk bottle to launch the rockets from, and set off the fireworks: Rockets, Jumpin' Jinnies, Catherine Wheels, Roman Candles. And we would all have sparklers, and, sometimes, the beautifully coloured Bengal Matches. We lit the sparklers patiently, from the candles in the hollowed-out turnip lanterns (which the English call 'swedes') – with the eyes, nose and a toothed mouth cut out. The lanterns had wire handles.

Sometimes the top of the turnip with a hole cut in as a chimney was put back on, and would make that great warm burning turnip smell that was an inseparable part of that great, heathen, death-acknowledging, life-affirming festival, that brightened up the approach of winter.

There was mischief too, at all times.

Some was nasty, like the bigger boys throwing bangers at groups of smaller children at Hallowe'en to scare them.

Some a harmless nuisance – like 'Thunder and Lightning' which could be played at any time of year and, at its simplest, was knocking on people's doors (like thunder) and running away (like lightning).

In its more sophisticated form, thread was used to secretly tie two facing neighbours' door-knockers together. Then another thread was tied in the middle, and we would hide at a distance and pull the end to knock both doors at once. The neighbours would come out simultaneously, look around and say, predictably enough, 'Those kids again!' or 'I'll give them thunder and lightning if I catch them!'

They could, of course, have found us easily enough, and

occasionally an individual victim with nothing better to do would venture from their doorstep and walk about looking for us – or even follow the trail of the thread if we hadn't wound it in. We would then have to escape through back gardens and hide until the coast was clear again. This could be a bit *too* exciting if the pursuer was particularly determined or grumpy. But we were never caught. Everybody's children did it anyway.

Easter was a much more dour and serious matter than Hallowe'en altogether.

Somehow there was a gloom on the earth at Easter – something between Death and Life. It only occasionally seemed to have the lightness of the approach of Spring. Otherwise it was all about killing a man on a cross. And if we were supposed to celebrate 'the Risen Christ', there wasn't much evidence of the good cheer of that. Easter seemed more like an Ulster Sunday that went on for too long.

Of course we had Easter eggs and the other good old country symbols of birth and fecundity. My father used to go and pick handfuls of whin flowers from the thorny bushes, and boil the eggs with them until the white shells were dyed sunshine yellow. Then we would all go to Musgrave Park, where there were newt ponds to look in, or Barnett's Park, where we could roll our eggs down the hill towards the River Lagan until they cracked, and were then peeled and eaten.

Not long after I started at Finaghy Primary School, our father made us hats for the Easter Bonnet competition. Mine was a crêpe paper covered, cardboard top hat, with cut-out rabbits and chicks that he had drawn stuck around the crown, and a banner between two sticks on the top; it probably said 'Happy Easter' or something like that. Anyway, I won a football – about as thrilling to me then as it would be now. So apart from a few rays of sunshine, Easter seemed mostly a miserable, dull grey time.

During his recovery from TB at the sanatorium, my father had learned, and still enjoyed, many new skills. The strangest was his ability to cut, twist, bend and drill clear and coloured perspex into all sorts of shapes and forms. I remember we had two or three twisted perspex table lamps, one with a bevelled, transparent green star as part of the stem. They were beautifully made, but never used, as I don't think he ever got round to wiring them.

He had, though, a constant urge to make things, and I remember his keenness to 'help' if I had a primary school project he could get involved in. I remember a miniature covered wagon he made from a cigar box he had got from somewhere – the shelter on top made from bent basket-willow hoops covered with unbleached linen, with drawstrings at the front and back. It was just like the ones in the westerns.

And, at another time, small carved birds on a twig, set in a wooden base, with pillow feathers for their wings, and carved matchwood for beaks.

Kind Mrs Johnson would look at these things brought in by the eager five year old, and say, 'Did your Daddy help you with this, David?' 'Yes, Mrs Johnson,' I would say, on the point of blushing, but proud nonetheless, as my father's latest creation was put on the classroom window sill for all to admire.

Apart from Easter, at other times of year bad weather didn't seem so bad. If you were allowed to have your friends in to play, or you had a toy that still gave you pleasure, you could feel snug and comfortable, whatever the weather. I had an old tin boat that Mrs Cooper, my Granda Gepp's neighbour in Euterpe Street, had given me – I think it had belonged to her son. You put a piece of 'meta-fuel', or meths, in a tray under a metal plate which had two pipes going to the back of the boat, and lit it. It used to *phut-phut* quite heartily round the bath. I haven't a clue how it worked.

Another real favourite, from the back of a Shredded Wheat packet I think, was a red printed cardboard cut-out that you folded into a plane and launched with an elastic band. I recall it flying beautifully, with heart-lifting loops and long graceful glides in the school playground.

Great fun, too, was a card and brown paper triangular thing, which came free with one of the comics – *The Eagle*, perhaps. This opened, with a really loud bang, when you swung it down from above your head.

Inside a cornflakes packet, some time in the Fifties, you got a small model of a nuclear submarine – but powered by baking soda. The *USS Nautilus* it was called. It was about two inches long, and came in blue or grey plastic. It had a black plug in the bottom with a hole in it. You put some baking soda in the space under the plug, put the plug back in, and gently put the submarine at the bottom of a bowl of water. Eventually it would rise to the surface, as the baking soda made a bubble that would bring it up. Then it would turn on its side, the bubble would come off, and the submarine would sink to the bottom and start the process all over again. It was a quiet pleasure for a dull day.

Of all the toys that had been bought for me, one of my favourite presents ever, oddly enough, was a simple torch – a 'bullseye' torch, with a thick glass lens in front, a green cracklepainted body, and the sort of flat battery with two brass terminals that made your tongue tingle if you licked them.

It seemed then that if you had your own light, you also had independence – otherwise the grown-ups decided when you were to be left in the dark.

Another torch I had was grey metal, and had red, clear and green lenses in a chrome slider on the front. This one was great for dramatic lighting under the table, and for signalling to friends, real and imagined, on dark evenings.

Unfortunately batteries were more expensive than pocket money allowed, and my torches always came to a sticky end when the overworked batteries leaked out that corrosive, blue-white gooey stuff.

If I were to tell you nothing else though, I would want to remember this:

In a darkened room sit four people – a mother and father with two children at their feet, laughing at the images thrown on a sheet pinned to the wall. There is a cartoon called *Noise Annoys Popeye* and a short film about two bear cubs playing in a German zoo, whose names I forget.

There is no sound with the films, only the clicking of a hand-cranked 9.5 mm projector (with its black crackle casing that was so strangely dry to the touch). Its lamp head leaks light in dust-moted beams as my father turns the handle.

Just that memory, and the sound – something like the aunts' treadle-driven Singer sewing machines – busy, but comforting.

And as my father cranks those two short films (all we ever

had) from one reel to the other – in that short laughter-filled time, before the window blind is put up again and the sheet unpinned from the picture rail, and the magic slowly dissipates – I am left with the gift of that sound in my memory, that frustratingly indescribable clock-clock-clock-clock-clock, that will somehow always define timeless innocence.

Eleven

WHEN I WAS ABOUT EIGHT YEARS old the protective wing of my older sister vanished, as Carole passed 'the Qualifying' and went on to a school near Dunmurry called Princess Gardens.

I don't think there was any connection (except that I now came home from school on my own) but at about this time I began to be bullied by a bigger and older schoolboy, who thought it was funny to steal my cap and soak it in the nearest muddy puddle. (We wore school caps and blazers with badges at primary school in those days.)

My father must have been recuperating from an operation at the time, as I remember he was there when I returned home, several days in a row, with a very wet and battered school cap.

School uniforms cost quite a lot of money, and my parents were by then very poor.

On the third or fourth occasion my father lost patience with his peace-loving son and told me that if the boy continued to push me around I had to hit him. My father was angry, and I said that I would, but more to appease him than out of any conviction.

Anyway, the next day I come home from school and my father sees my muddy cap and says, 'Well, did you hit him?' 'Yes,' I lie, hoping he won't ask for any details, or I'll have to make them up pretty quick. Just at this point Carole arrives back from her new school with a schoolfriend. 'Oh, Mr Gepp,' says the schoolfriend, 'you should have seen what your David did to that big boy from Garron Crescent – he's gone running home crying to his Mammy.' I was open-mouthed with admiration for this girl – I hardly knew her. How did she know the trouble I was in with my father? And she'd made it so convincing.

I was grateful to her – I didn't stop to think about why she should help a small boy she'd only just met.

I don't know if it was weeks or months, or longer, that it took me to put the ill-tasting truth together.

Of course she'd been convincing, she was only telling what she'd seen.

I'd lost my temper with that boy for fear of my father, and when I'd done it I had denied it so strongly to myself that I'd lost all memory of it.

And the real irony of it was that when I was *lying* about it I was really telling the *truth*. (It still bothers me, that one – on a

practical as much as a philosophical basis – how many people
have I beaten up and forgotten about it?)

Until about that time the only television I had seen was in the
home of some friends or very distant relatives of my parents.
They lived in Finaghy Road South and their house was
detached or semi-detached (it was big compared to ours,
anyway).

In the dark wooden entrance hall, by the umbrella stands,
they had a full-sized dog, which I thought was stuffed, but was
really some sort of eccentric Victorian toy that barked loudly
when you pulled its lead.

I was about the same age as the daughter of the house, and
we would watch *Children's Hour* on their small blue-green
screen.

From the moment the Crystal Palace transmitter picture
appeared with its radiating circles, at the start of *Children's
Newsreel*, I absorbed the information eagerly and uncritically.
I remember an 'expert' talking about Nelson's sea mug and
explaining why it had a porcelain toad, or frog, halfway down
the inside. It was so that Nelson, drinking his tea, would jump
when its head poked out and think, 'Goodness, I'd better get
on with the battle!'

Educationally *Children's Newsreel* was of the same sort of reliability as the boys' comics I read around this time – the *Buster, Beezer, Rover* or *Hotspur* – which I would get by swapping the *Beano* or *Dandy*. I also got the *Topper* sometimes, and, my favourite, the *Eagle* (with Dan Dare and the Mekon).

The *Rover* carried 'informative' items in a line or two at the bottom of each page – 'If Britain's coastline was a straight line it would stretch all the way to Calcutta' – that sort of thing. I soaked it all up.

My credulity was shattered, though, when I read that Belfast City Council had replaced all the lamp posts with rubber ones, as so many had been knocked over by motorists.

So I realised somebody was just having a laugh and writing whatever came into their heads to amuse themselves. I suppose they thought Belfast was too far away from the centre of Empire (the 'Home' counties) for it to matter. The experience sowed the seeds of a healthy scepticism, or caution at least, in believing everything I read, watched or listened to. At least there was still Mr Pastry ...

At home we had a big old mahogany, cathedral-shaped wireless, with cut-out church window shapes, covered from behind with fawn-coloured fabric. If you put your eyes close to the fabric you could see through to the glowing valves. It took some time to warm up and smelled of scorching dust while it did. It had a wire aerial with some kind of small metal box, attached with screw terminals, which I suppose improved the reception.

We had the choice of the Light, the Third, or the Home programmes on the BBC, or Radio Luxembourg. We would listen to *The Clitheroe Kid*, *The McCooeys* (which I loved) on the BBC, and *Irish Family Favourites* on Radio Luxembourg.

On Irish Family Favourites they played all the old Percy French songs, and it was as cosy as Val Doonican's cardigan, before he was old enough to have one. There was another song that went something like:

> She was a fine big lump
> Of an a-ggeri-cultural Irish girl ...
> The full of your arms of Irish love
> Was Katie-Anne Magee

Similarly, when my Granda Roberts had first met the young woman he was to marry, ' ... he could hardly get his arms around her' – which he thought was a very desirable quality in a wife.

That she had been forced to work as a servant since childhood and couldn't read or write was something he would try, and fail, to correct later. For the wide, open world was her schoolroom, and, when he sat her down to tutor, she would say, 'Ach, come on Joe, let's get out for a walk instead!'

So when my mother – her fifth child – was born, it was still 'Lizzie Roberts, her mark' in bureaucratic copperplate on the birth certificate – and still is today – beside the very precise, lightly marked X-shape that was hers alone.

I look at it now, and feel a fond connection to this forebear of mine, who died before I was born and about whom I know so very little.

So now, in spite of – or perhaps because of – my grandmother's inability to read or write, I find myself wondering why Ireland (the whole island) has a culture so much more deeply literary than visual. In the beginning was the word ... then the music ...

Now when I think of the Belfast I grew up in, it is a part of the literature – the word, rooted in the day-to-day speech of people there – that I miss the most.

The strange perfection of a phrase like 'I'm feeling a bit through-other' to describe the slightly alienated stage of being ill, or sickening for something. Many of these turns of speech echo in my mind – and I feel cheered, or wistful, sad or amused, but mostly homesick – when I hear these voices from my past.

And I am annoyed, and feel somehow polluted by exile, when I find myself using the ugly English of 'Aren't I?' ('Yes, of course I are') more often than the 'Amn't I?' of my childhood.

I miss too those elegant, emphasising refrains:

It's a quare big house, *so it is* ...
They went to Bangor, *so they did* ...
I love potato bread, *so I do* ...
They were starving, *so they were* ...
We do it that way too, *so we do* ...

And the simple idiosyncrasies like:

It happened there now ...
She's a wee dote ...
He's a geg ...
It was only a wee toady thing ...
Child dear, would you have a wee titter of wit ...

And the reporting of simple dramas in the third person:

Here's me: 'I'm not doing that'
Here's ma mammy: 'You'll do that or I'll tell your
            daddy'
Here's ma daddy: 'What are you two on about?'

Or:

see me
see ma mammy
see bacon
I hate it

When Granda got his television I remember watching programmes like *Danger Man*, *The Munsters*, *The Flintstones*, and *Hiram Halliday* (which was a comedy I loved, about a very geeky secret agent who always won out in the end).

When I was about nine or ten I was at Granda's one evening and began to get a pain in the back of my head – I don't remember much more, later I was told that my body went rigid and I had gone into a fever. I have no sense of the time. They got me home somehow, and the doctor for me. But I don't know whether it was hours or days before I came round again. There are two events I remember from the strange place that fever took me to.

Both are in a deep, silent space:

In the first I am floating away from a beautifully made, portholed, mahogany and brass flying saucer, and I have the most heartfelt sense of loss. I'm drifting towards the planet Earth, and somehow know I am leaving all that I love behind with the spaceship.

I have never known such a profound sadness or longing, before or since – and yet with such a strange, strong sense of purpose, or necessity, or even Fate ...

In the second 'dream', which has more of the quality of hallucination, I'm looking at the blue globe that is the Earth – and then it splits in two, like an apple, into black space and begins to fall from my field of view. In an oppressive, deafening silence I scream in horror – and I am back in bed screaming for my Mammy. I think that image of terrible loss scared me back to life again.

So I came back down to earth, and life resumed.

I sat 'the Qualifying' and passed.

I still have the bone-handled knife that my parents gave me as a present. I saw it in the window of a shop in Cornmarket and had wanted it for ages. They said they would buy it for me if I passed the exam – though if I had failed I think they would have given it to me as consolation!

The brass inserts in the handle are covered with verdigris now, and the blade is pitted and crusted with rust, but I can still make out details of leaves and the feet of the deer that used to run through the imaginary landscape that was engraved on it, and made me want to own it for this romance.

Norman, my best friend, failed the examination, and went to Larkfield Intermediate, near Dunmurry. I, however, was now 'qualified' to go to a grammar school. And so we two friends were separated by the system, and saw less and less of one another until we inhabited two worlds that scarcely overlapped.

So now, many decades later, I think of Norman and his elder sister Margaret (who used to make us 'tea' and smother the digestive biscuits with butter) and his brother Albert and his pretty young wife, and of how the war that was to come would affect them. And I wonder whether they stayed in Belfast, or if they travelled abroad looking for solace, for refuge – for the body or the mind – from that tortured and twisted place.

And do they find themselves in exile at this time of peace? And does their heart, like mine, ache for its home?

> And what a man is born to, both the place,
> Where'er it be, that hath received his being
> Out of oblivion, and given his mind
> The shapes and hues of earth, the sights of heaven,
> The place whence he sets forth to meet strange things,
> Whither returns to find his own, himself;
> This bides, the harbour of his fancy – and draws him
> Spite of all else from world's end to world's end.

Robert Bridges,
The Return of Ulysses, Act II, ll. 845-52

ABOUT DAVID GEPP

David Gepp was born in 1948 in Belfast and grew up on a predominantly Protestant, working-class housing estate on the western outskirts of the city. He left school at 17 and took work – in what would now be called a gap year – in a laboratory at the ICI plant at Kilroot. He found ICI 'the chemical Brobdingnagian' – based near the site of Jonathan Swift's church on the shores of Belfast Lough – busily filling the streams with molten plastic. Sceptical by then anyway 'of the social value of Terylene', Gepp experienced a polar shift in his sensibilities and moved towards the Arts – the gap year expanding exponentially. After a spell in London in the later 60s 'as an apprentice, and then a fully qualified, hippy' he went to Nottingham College of Art.

He worked at the first Glastonbury Festival and at the free festival on the Isle of Wight. (Where he remembers the privilege of 'listening on a dark night to the windblown soaring of Jimi Hendrix' last ever set', at the end of August 1970.) Hendrix' death shortly afterwards 'seemed like a metaphor for the death of the hippy movement'.

Gepp returned to Belfast in the early 70s, where he swept streets for a time, before becoming involved in a street theatre project for children, 'travelling to different parts of the city in a double-decker bus driven by a really nice, big trans-gendered lorry driver in a frock' and entertaining children with an interactive programme loosely based on Tolkien's *Lord of the Rings*. He met his future (first) wife at this time, and moved some time afterwards to Donegal 'as a sort of refugee'. There he spent an impoverished winter 'surviving only by the help of friends and kind neighbours'. He was also, unknowingly, suffering the symptoms of what would later be recognised as PTSD. He moved to Wales and in 1979 became a student on the formative Creative Photography course at Derby, where he was taught by John Blakemore and Paul Hill. Divorce interrupted the third year of his studies and Gepp returned to his then home in the uplands of Wales. In 1983 he met Merlyn Hancock. They were married in 1985. With her support and advice Gepp began to receive commissions, and grant funding from the Arts Council of Wales. This allowed him to realise major personal photographic projects, including 'The Narrow Road to the Deep North/Auguries of Innocence', exhibited at the Ulster Museum in 1997. Gepp's work in Belfast and in Venice became the subject of Clive Flowers' critically acclaimed BBC documentary, 'An Italian Dream' (shown again as part of the Belfast Photo Festival 2011).

Gepp became an Associate Lecturer at Hereford College of Arts, and taught on the BA Hons (Photography) course, which he helped initiate, until returning to Ireland. He continues as a visiting lecturer, and working on self-directed projects. He is a vegan and lives near the western coast of Donegal with his wife Merlyn and their dogs, Yin and Yang.

ABOUT THE COVER ART WORK

'Lagan Mud' is about memory, antiquity, chaos and nostalgia – the 'long ache' of homesickness known as *hiraeth* in Welsh. It is a layered photogram (approximately 8'x 6') made with light-sensitised mud taken from the River Lagan near Belfast – literally my home ground.

David Gepp